Churches to Visit in Scotland 1998

PUBLISHED BY

Scotland's Churches Scheme

WITH ILLUSTRATIONS BY

JOHN R. HUME

CLARENCE HOUSE
S. W. 1

Her Majesty Queen Elizabeth
The Queen Mother as Patron of
Scotland's Churches Scheme
has spent a happy time looking
at the charming drawings of the churches
and is confident that the book will do
much to enhance the importance
of the Scheme in the eyes
of the public.

Her Majesty looks forward to
seeing the 1998 edition.

Office: Dunedin, Holehouse Rd, Eaglesham, Glasgow G76 0JF
Tel: 01355 302416 Fax: 01355 303181
Web site: http: //churchnet.ucsm.ac.uk/scotchurch/
Registered Charity No. SC 022868

Front cover: Angel Window, The Church of the Holy Rude, Stirling
watercolour by John R. Hume OBE

Designed by Dalrymple
Typeset in Monotype Columbus
Printed by Mackenzie & Storrie Ltd
Published by Scotland's Churches Scheme

A C.I.P. record for this title is available from the British Library
ISBN 0 9525 336 3 4

PREFACE

From the President

Lady Marion Fraser LT MA LLD

In three years Scotland's Churches Scheme has become a valued feature in our national life. People find renewed vigour in their own congregations as they become more closely involved in the wider life of the community. Ever more church doors throughout Scotland are opening in this fresh Ministry of Welcome. Our attractive guidebook is complimented on its wealth of information and its shelf appeal wherever it is found.

As we move confidently towards the Millennium our thanks go to all those who have made our vision a practical reality. We value greatly the generous funding that many Trusts, individual benefactors and National Agencies have given us. Without their encouragement we could have achieved little, and I can assure them that their generosity is deeply appreciated by our Trustees as well as by those who tell us how much the Scheme means to them ... peaceful places to rest and reflect, a new interest in our architectural and ecclesiastical heritage, warm friendliness from those who make the Scheme work so effectively at grass roots level.

We look to all of you who care about this nation-wide Churches' initiative to spread the good news so that we can attract the interest and sustaining financial support which will allow us to build confidently on our established knowledge and to develop the Scheme for the benefit of all who love and need our rich church heritage.

Information on other properties
and sites open to visitors may be obtained from:

HISTORIC SCOTLAND
Longmore House, Salisbury Place, Edinburgh EH9 1SH

THE NATIONAL TRUST FOR SCOTLAND
5 Charlotte Square, Edinburgh EH2 4DR

SCOTLAND'S GARDENS SCHEME
31 Castle Terrace, Edinburgh EH1 2EL

DOORS OPEN DAY
The Scottish Civic Trust, 24 George Square, Glasgow G2 1EF

THE SCOTTISH TOURIST BOARD
23 Ravelston Terrace
Edinburgh EH4 3EU

Welcome to Scotland's Churches Scheme 1998. For the past sixteen hundred years the history of religion has mirrored the history of Scotland. It is a fascinating story, characterised by faith, ambition, achievement, devotion and confrontation! This guide will lead you through our ecclesiastical history and prompt you to visit some of the buildings and discover the story of the people who helped shape the Scottish nation.

Today visitors to Scotland's churches will find a peaceful experience and a warm welcome at all the buildings listed within this guide. Scotland's churches reflect a rich architectural and cultural inheritance and with the information of Scotland's Churches Scheme many of these treasures are available for all to enjoy.

There are even more churches in the 1998 guide. In 1997 over 90 new churches joined the Scheme, bringing the total number to over 400. I should like to thank the Trustees of Scotland's Churches Scheme and the participating congregations for developing this initiative, ensuring its continued growth and success, and opening their doors to the visitor.

This guide will become indispensable to everyone wanting to explore Scotland's ecclesiastical heritage.

TOM BUNCLE

Chief Executive, Scottish Tourist Board

FOREWORD

'Block City'

by Robert Louis Stevenson (from A Child's Garden of Verses*)*

What are you able to build with your blocks?
Castles and palaces, temples and docks.
Rain may keep raining, and others go roam,
But I can be happy and building at home.

Let the sofa be mountains, the carpet be sea,
There I'll establish a city for me;
A kirk and a mill and a palace beside,
And a harbour as well where my vessels may ride.

Great is the palace with pillar and wall,
A sort of a tower on the top of it all,
And steps coming down in an orderly way
To where my toy vessels lie safe in the bay.

This one is sailing and that one is moored:
Hark to the song of the sailors on board!
And see on the steps of my palace, the kings
Coming and going with presents and things!

Now I have done it, down let it go!
All in a moment the town is laid low.
Block upon block lying scattered and free
What is there left of my town by the sea?

Yet as I saw it, I see it again,
The kirk and the palace, the ships and the men;
And long as I live, and where'er I may be,
I'll always remember my town by the sea.

Where we live, and among what we live, shapes the minds of Scots more consciously, when it comes to what we are currently supposed to call the built environment, than that of most nations, save perhaps the Italians and the Czechs. Our architectural inheritance is so eccentric, various, compressed within the small but wild spread of our land that it comes, against our decisive landscapes, Lowland, Highland, Island, volcanic, riverine, to express our mental and social habits. Nowhere perhaps is this more explicit than in the architecture of our churches.

I'm no professional, either of architecture or of the Church. My only claim to your kind attention is that I am the daughter of my father, Colin McWilliam. It was in his company that I first got the feel for buildings, and a reduplicated feel for religious buildings. I hope I am not too much repeating myself – I've mentioned these places elsewhere, if only translated in fiction – if I tell you of a few we visited together. the point of mentioning them is to show the extraordinary variety of the places and forms of sanctity our country offers, often to those who least expect to be surprised in the way they are surprised, moved aesthetically, intellectually, spiritually, even inarticulably, by these constructions of human ability and aspiration.

When I was small, my father took me to church at a smoky, high Piscy place by Carrubbers Close, Old St Paul's. Its greatly resonant name dropped fully into my consciousness only decades later, when I read the works of W. Harrison Ainsworth. As a schoolgirl, I attended carol services at St Giles; the crumbling flags moved us as we stirred in slow march, holding candles. I attended the cathedral Church of St Mary's and the Canongate Kirk, white and blue as a Scandinavian kitchen; my father was ecumenical, fair, almost exhaustingly unpartisan. I felt ashamed to be tugged between appearances, knew I should respond only to the transparency of goodness, not the manufactured shell of beauty. But in plainness I saw beauty too, and the worshipfulness of work even in things fancier.

When he was in his middle thirties, and I about nine, he took me to the Cathedral of the Isles on Great Cumbrae. It reared up among freezing daffodils, beautiful, serious, completely worth the journey over choppy water for a fractious child.

The Greyfriars Kirk is perhaps the most intimate place of my childhood churchyard wanderings alone; he never took me there. I just go there, because there he is, in the Flodden Wall, reserved for distinguished Scots, where I am sure he never thought he would be; for my father was one of those rare beings, a devout sceptical, intelligent aesthete who was never vain and therefore didn't once envisage his own funeral, a habit almost caricaturably common to us all.

I'm vain and I was christened at Rosslyn Chapel; with the Piccolomini Chapel in Sienna's Duomo, it's the oddest, most laminated little sacred place you could enter.

This book will provide for you something of what my father's company provided for me; in addition, it offers detail that my faulty memory cannot. Reference books such as this, informed by a conscientious love of detail and by generosity, supply something elsewhere not to be found – a gentle companion in the quest for knowledge, a companion always offering more, and leading on to the next place. Among the close turfed stones of the island chapels, the lush wet slopes of Border kirks or the whistling sky-filled vaults of the gutted Abbeys, there is something, no matter whether or what you do or do not believe, to be heard and learned.

HOW TO USE THIS GUIDE

Entries are arranged alphabetically by council and then by locality. The number preceding each entry refers to the map on the fold-out back cover. The denomination of the church is shown on the last line of each entry, followed by the relevant symbols:

- Access for partially abled
- Hearing induction loop for the deaf
- Welcomers and guides on duty
- Guidebooks and souvenirs
- Exhibition
- Features for children / link with schools
- Church Recorders at work
- Refreshments
- WC Toilets on premises
- **A** Category A Listing
- **B** Category B Listing
- **C** Category C Listing

CATEGORY A: Buildings of national or more than local importance, either architectural or historic, or fine little-altered examples of some particular period, style or type.

CATEGORY B: Buildings of regional or more than local importance, or major examples of some particular period, style or building type which may have been altered.

CATEGORY C: Buildings of local importance, or lesser examples of any period style, or building type, as originally constructed or altered; and simple traditional buildings which group well with others.

The information appearing in the gazetteer of this guidebook is supplied by the participating churches. While this is believed to be correct at the time of going to press, Scotland's Churches Scheme cannot accept any responsibility for its accuracy.

· Aberdeen ·

1 THE CATHEDRAL OF OUR LADY OF THE ASSUMPTION

Huntly Street, Aberdeen

The principal church of the Roman Catholic Diocese of Aberdeen, built in 1860, Alexander Ellis. Spire and bells added in 1877, designed by R.G. Wilson. Contains religious artefacts by Charles Blakeman, Gabriel Loire, Ann Davidson, Felix McCullough, David Gulland and Alexander Brodie. The organ is a rare example of the work of James Connacher, Huddersfield, 1887. Off Union Street. Mass Times Vigil Saturday 7pm, Sunday 8am, 11.15am, 6pm

OPEN DAILY SUMMER 8AM–5PM,
WINTER 8AM–4PM

Also Aberdeen Doors Open Day.
Clergy House at 20 Huntly Street

Roman Catholic WC B

The Cathedral of Our Lady of the Assumption, Aberdeen

2 THE CHAPEL OF THE CONVENT OF ST MARGARET OF SCOTLAND

17 Spital, Aberdeen

The chapel, built in 1892, is one of the earliest works of Sir Ninian Comper, son of the Revd John Comper, Rector of St John's Church in Aberdeen, who in 1863 had invited sisters from St Margaret's Convent, East Grinstead to work with him. The furnishings, fittings and windows were also designed by Sir Ninian, and executed in his workshop. The oak panelling over the stalls was a thank offering after the Second World War. On left hand side of road from Mounthooly roundabout to the Old Town. Services: Vespers 5.30pm (Thursdays, 5pm), daily Eucharist at varying times, please tel 01224 632648 for exact information

OPEN BY ARRANGEMENT

Apply at front door of convent. Chapel may be viewed through grille in west porch

Scottish Episcopal A

3 FERRYHILL PARISH CHURCH

Fonthill Road, Aberdeen

Designed by Duncan McMillan, 1874, in Early Gothic style with a tall square bell tower with octagonal spire. The side galleries and organ were added in 1896. The sanctuary was re-ordered, 1994 by Oliver Humphries. Memorial windows: Courage and Victory by W. Moore after the First World War, Piper Alpha window by Jane Bayliss, 1994. Allen organ, 1994. At junction of Fonthill Road and Polmuir Road. Sunday Service 11am, for other Services see notice board

OPEN WEEKDAY MORNINGS DURING SCHOOL TERM TIMES

Other times by arrangement tel Mr Sherriffs 01224 584484

Church of Scotland WC B

4 GILCOMSTON SOUTH CHURCH

Union Street, Aberdeen

Sandstone and granite building by William Smith, 1868. Spire added in 1875 and rebuilt in 1995. Stained glass by David Gauld, Douglas Strachan and Jane Bayliss. Oak screen and choir stalls. Binns pipe organ, 1902. 100 yards from west end of Union Street. Sunday Services 11am and 7pm, Wednesday 7.30pm, Saturday Prayer Meeting 7pm

OPEN ABERDEEN DOORS OPEN DAY

Other times contact Prof Lyall, 6 Beechgrove Avenue, Aberdeen tel 01224 635704

Church of Scotland WC C

5 KIRK OF ST NICHOLAS

Back Wynd, Aberdeen

The 'Mither Kirk' of Aberdeen dates from the 12th century. The present building is largely 18th and 19th-century, The west end 1755, by James Gibbs, the east end by Archibald Simpson, 1837. The church contains the Chapel of the Oil Industry, and the 15th-century St Mary's Chapel. The carillon of 48 bells is the largest in Great Britain. 17th-century embroidered wall hangings. Situated in Aberdeen city centre. Sunday Service 11am, also July and August 9.30am, Daily Prayers Monday to Friday 1.05pm

OPEN 1 MAY–30 SEPTEMBER MONDAY TO FRIDAY 12 NOON–4PM, SATURDAY 1–3PM

Other times on application to the Church Office 10am–1pm

Church of Scotland WC A

6 NEWHILLS CHURCH

Bucksburn, Aberdeen

The present church was built in 1830 to a design by Archibald Simpson, near to the site of the original 17th-century church (now part of the graveyard). Painted coat of arms of the patron, Lord James Hay of Easton, Earl of Fife and several modern banners add colour to the interior. Sunday Service 10.30am and 6pm (not July and August)

OPEN MONDAY TO FRIDAY 9AM–1PM

Church of Scotland (by arrangement) WC C

7 ROSEMOUNT CHURCH

120 Rosemount Place, Aberdeen

Traditional church, 1870, converted to multi-purpose Celebration Centre in 1984. Ground floor accommodates Sunday worship, weekday activities and coffee lounge. Gallery houses 'Jonah's Journey' – children's museum. Situated close to two municipal parks. By road or by bus 22 from lower end of Union Street. Sunday Service 11am

OPEN ALL YEAR (NOT PUBLIC HOLIDAYS) MONDAY TO SATURDAY 10AM–12 NOON, SUNDAY 2.30–4.30PM (EXCEPT JULY)

Church of Scotland WC C

8 ST ANDREW'S CATHEDRAL

King Street, Aberdeen

Built by Archibald Simpson, 1817 and altered and enhanced by Sir Ninian Comper, 1939–45. Gold burnished baldacchino over the high altar. National memorial to Samuel Seabury, first Bishop of America consecrated in Aberdeen in 1784. Interesting roof heraldry depicting American states and Jacobite supporters of the '45 rebellion. Stained glass. Sir John Betjeman described it as one of Aberdeen's best modern buildings. 3-manual organ by Hill, Norman & Beard, recently restored. Services Holy Communion 8am, Sung Eucharist 10.15am, Evensong 6.30pm

OPEN MAY–SEPTEMBER MONDAY TO SATURDAY 10AM–4PM

Scottish Episcopal ♿ ⸎ ⌂ ☕ wc **A**

9 ST COLUMBA'S PARISH CHURCH

Braehead Way, Bridge of Don

St Columba's Parish Church is shared with the local Roman Catholic congregation. The most notable feature is a steel cross at rear of the church. Sunday Services 10am & 6.30pm

OPEN BY ARRANGEMENT

Contact Mr Thompson tel 01224 703753

Church of Scotland ♿ ⸎ ② ☕ wc

St Columba's Parish Church, Bridge of Don

10 ST MACHAR'S CATHEDRAL

The Chanonry, Aberdeen

14th–16th-century nave with unique heraldic ceiling and fortified west front. Interesting monuments, stained glass. Ruined transepts. Peal of eight bells. Sunday Services 11am & 6pm

OPEN DAILY 9AM–5PM

Recitals programme information tel 01224 485988

e-mail stmachar@ifb.co.uk web: www.ifb.net/stmachar

Church of Scotland ♿ ⸎ ☐ ⌂ ② wc **A**

11 ST MARGARET OF SCOTLAND

Gallowgate, Aberdeen

Completed in 1869, the spacious sanctuary includes many fine examples of the work of Sir Ninian Comper, including the chapel of St Nicholas, the first building he designed and with the original stained glass. His style is mainly Early English with elements of Byzantine and Renaissance. Memorial garden. Just north of Marischal College. Sunday Services Low Mass 9.15am, Parish Mass 10.30am, Evensong 6pm, Folk Mass 7.30pm

OPEN TUESDAY MORNINGS

Other times contact Canon Nimmo tel 01224 644969 or A. Allan tel 01224 872960

Gallowgate Festival Saturday in Early August

Scottish Episcopal ♿ ⸎ ⸎ ⌂ **B**

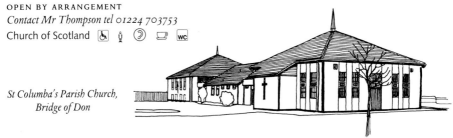

12 ST MARY'S CHURCH

Carden Place, Aberdeen

The variety of granites and patterned roof tiles earned it the nickname 'The Tartan Kirkie'. To a design by Alexander Ellis and the Revd George Lee, dating from 1864. The east end sustained severe damage during an air raid in April, 1943. Reconstructed, 1952. The church is home to a Samuel Green chamber organ, built in 1778. On the left between Skene Street and Queen's Road. Sunday Service 8am and 10.15am, Tuesday 7pm, Wednesday 11am

OPEN BY ARRANGEMENT

Contact the Rector tel 01224 584123

Scottish Episcopal (hearing loop) WC A

· Aberdeenshire ·

13 ST TERNAN'S CHURCH, ARBUTHNOTT NO8074

Almost certainly a St Ternan cult church long before it became a parish church by the late 12th century. The chancel dates from the early 13th century, the Arbuthnott family aisle and the bell-tower from the late 15th century and the nave is medieval or earlier but has been much altered. The church was gutted by fire in 1889 and reopened in 1890 with the nave and chancel restored as at the time of consecration in 1242; the architect for the restoration was A. Marshall Mackenzie. The unique Arbuthnott Missal, Psalter and Prayer Book (now in Paisley Museum) were transcribed and illuminated in the Priest's Room above the Arbuthnott Aisle between 1497 and 1500. On the B967, 3 miles from Inverbervie. For Services, see local paper and notice board

St Ternan's Church, Arbuthnott

OPEN ALL YEAR

Refreshments in Grassic Gibbon Centre in village

Church of Scotland (wheelchair access) (guide) A

14 BIRSE AND FEUGHSIDE PARISH CHURCH, BALLOGIE NO5795

Ballogie, near Banchory

Dates from 12th century. Link with Crusades. 17th-century graveyard. United with Finzean and Strachan. Sunday Service 11am July

OPEN MAY–SEPTEMBER MONDAY TO FRIDAY 10AM–4PM

Church of Scotland (wheelchair access) WC B

15 BANFF PARISH CHURCH NJ6863

High Street, Banff

Built in 1789, with tower added in 1839. Chancel added and interior altered in 1929. Stained glass. Small chapel created at rear of church in 1994. Pulpit, font, communion table and stained glass in chancel all gifted in 1929. Other furnishings from Trinity & Alvah Church, united in 1994. Beside St Mary's car park. Sunday Services 11am, September–June 6pm

OPEN MID-JUNE TO AUGUST 10AM–12 NOON, 2–4PM

Also Doors Open Day September

Church of Scotland A

16 ST JAMES'S CHURCH, CRUDEN BAY

Chapel Hill, Cruden Bay

The tall spire of St James's can be seen from miles around. Designed by William Hay in 1842. The font from the chantry chapel, built after the battle between the Scots and the Danes in 1012. 1½ miles from Cruden Bay. Sunday Service Family Communion 9.30am

OPEN DAILY 10AM TIL DUSK

Scottish Episcopal B

17 ST MARY ON THE ROCK, ELLON

Craighall, Ellon

A superb example of the work of George Edmund Street, built in 1871 to incorporate chancel, nave, narthex and spire. Floor tiles by Minton. Good glass, including windows by Clayton & Bell on the north side of the nave, Lavers & Barreau on the south side, all dating from the 1880's and by Jane Bayliss, 1996. On the A90/A948, at the south end of the town. Sunday Service Eucharist 8.30am, Family Communion 11.15am

OPEN DAILY 10AM TIL DUSK

Scottish Episcopal A

Birse and Feughside Parish Church, Ballogie

18 FINTRY PARISH CHURCH

Fintry Village

The present church, built in 1823, was constructed around the original kirk of 1642, and the congregation continued to worship in the old sanctuary while building went on around them!

On completion, the inner church was demolished. The bell was transferred from old to new and is still in use today. Early 20th-century stained glass, including a First World War memorial window. Session House in the kirkyard added 1992. Sunday Service 10am

OPEN EASTER SATURDAY AND MAY TO SEPTEMBER SATURDAY 2–4PM

Church of Scotland B

19 BERVIE PARISH CHURCH, INVERBERVIE NO8272

43 King Street, Inverbervie

Built in 1836 with elegant clock and bell tower. Two stained glass windows originally from United Free Church. Hammond organ, 1904. In centre of town. Sunday Service 11.30am

OPEN BY ARRANGEMENT

Contact Mr W. Beattie, 39 King Street tel 01561 361256 or 9 Farquhar Street tel 01561 362728

Church of Scotland WC B

Bervie Parish Church, Inverbervie

20 ST PHILIP'S, CATTERLINE NO8678

St Ninian was reputed to have landed at Catterline. The present building, designed by Charles Brand, dates from 1848 and was built on the site of an earlier church, retaining its historic graveyard. The style is Early English. The interior has been recently refurbished. Off A9 between Montrose and Stonehaven and near Dunottar Castle. Sunday Services 9.30 Holy Communion second and last Sundays in month

OPEN BY ARRANGEMENT

Contact Mr Reid tel 01569 750360

Scottish Episcopal C

21 FINZEAN CHURCH NO5993

Finzean, near Banchory

Small mission church. United with Birse and Strachan. Between Banchory & Aboyne on South Deeside Road. Sunday Service 11am June and September

OPEN MAY–SEPTEMBER MONDAY TO FRIDAY 10AM–4PM

Church of Scotland B

22 ST DROSTAN, INSCH NJ6228

Alexander Ross, 1894. Agreeable rustic Gothic in red granite with sandstone dressings. Red-tiled roof with broach-spired wooden bellcote. Font, 1892, and screen, 1904. Church is on road from Insch railway station to town centre. B992 off A96. Service 2nd & 4th Sundays Sung Eucharist 10am

OPEN BY ARRANGEMENT

Contact Mrs Mitchell, Greenhaugh, Rannes Street, Insch tel 01464 820276

Scottish Episcopal **C**

23 KING DAVID OF SCOTLAND EPISCOPAL CHURCH, INVERBERVIE NO8272

Victoria Terrace, Inverbervie

Small, simple church with very pretty interior. Shared with the local Roman Catholic community. Sunday Service 9.30am Holy Communion. Roman Catholic Mass Saturday 6.30pm

OPEN DAILY 9AM–4.30PM

Scottish Episcopal

24 MACDUFF PARISH CHURCH NJ7064

Church Street, Macduff

Once used to guide boats to safe haven,this white box kirk of 1805 high on the bluff above the harbour was transformed in 1865 by architect James Matthews of Aberdeen into a magnificent Italianate landmark, with notable stained glass windows and a lovely 3-storey tower with a lead-domed roof and cupola above. Loft galleried interior, most of the fittings date from 1865. Magnificent views. Nearby stand the town cross and an anchor, symbolic of the message of the church. Sunday Services 11am & 6pm

OPEN BY ARRANGEMENT

Contact tel 01261 833905

Church of Scotland ♿ 👂 WC **B**

25 ST MATTHEW & ST GEORGE, OLDMELDRUM NJ8127

Ross & Joass, 1863. Pleasing granite Early Decorated with striking chequered voussoirs to west window. Octagonal spire alongside the simple nave and chancel. Tendril-like freestone tracery is carved with real freedom. Stained glass by Hardman records the Life of Our Lord. Intricate Arts & Crafts monument to Beauchamp Colclough Urquhart of Meldrum. Church is at the north end of the village on A947. Sunday Service: 11.30am

OPEN BY ARRANGEMENT

Contact the Rector tel 01651 872208

Scottish Episcopal ♿ **B**

St Matthew & St George, Oldmeldrum

26 OLD SEMINARY, SCALAN

Braes of Glenlivet, Ballindalloch

Scalan (Gaelic for a turf-roofed shelter) is a plain 18th-century house, the most significant relic of 'penal days'. Built in 1717 as a seminary for the training of priests. Turn off B9008 Tomintoul to Dufftown at Pole Inn (signposted). Annual Mass 1st Sunday July 4pm

OPEN ALL YEAR

Roman Catholic **B**

27 ST JAMES THE GREAT, STONEHAVEN NO8786

Arbuthnott Street, Stonehaven

The nave was built by Sir Robert Rowand Anderson in 1877 in Norman/Early English style. The chancel was added in 1885 and the narthex and baptistry in 1906 by Arthur Clyne. Baptistry glass by Ninian Comper, 1929, elaborately sculptured reredos by Gambier-Parry of London. Off south side of Market Square in Stonehaven. Sunday Services 8.30 & 10.30am, Thursday 10.30am

OPEN EASTER TO END SEPTEMBER MONDAYS—FRIDAYS 2—4PM

Scottish Episcopal ♿ 📖 WC **A**

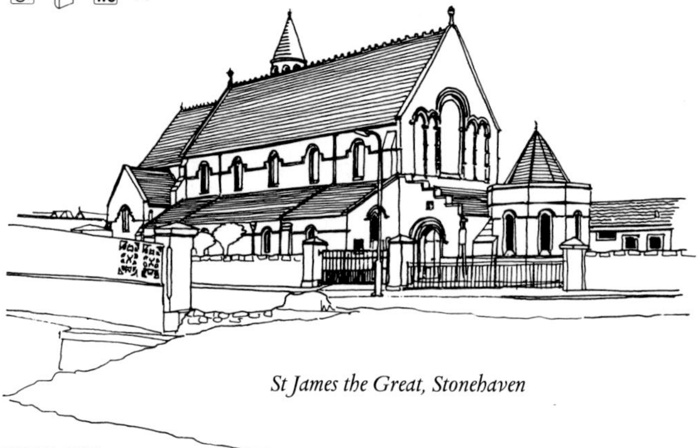

St James the Great, Stonehaven

28 STRACHAN CHURCH NO6792

Strachan, near Banchory

Situated on old drove road. Ancient graveyard. United with Birse and Finzean. Between Banchory & Aboyne on South Deeside Road. Sunday Service 11am May and August

OPEN MAY—SEPTEMBER MONDAY TO FRIDAY 10AM—4PM

Church of Scotland **C**

29 ALL SAINTS', WHITERASHES NJ8523

Gothic style Nave and chancel built by James Matthews in 1858. Windows by Ninian Comper of saints chosen for the Christian names of the Irvines of Drum & Straloch. On A947, 3 miles south of Oldmeldrum. Service 1st Sunday, Evensong 3pm

OPEN BY ARRANGEMENT

Contact the Rector tel 01651 872208

Scottish Episcopal ♿ (one step) **B**

30 ALL SAINTS', WOODHEAD OF FETTERLETTER NJ7838

Early English aisleless nave and chancel by John Henderson, 1849. The fine tower with the slated broach spire was added in 1870. Described by Pratt in *Buchan* as "one of the finest examples of a Scottish village church". Crosses and a sheaf of arrows from Fyvie Priory are incorporated in the walls. The altar and reredos are from St Margaret's, Forgue. 1½ miles east of Fyvie. Services 1st & 3rd Sundays 10.15am

OPEN BY ARRANGEMENT

Contact Mrs Cleaver, Gowanlea, Woodhead tel 01651 891513

Scottish Episcopal **B**

· Angus ·

31 ST VIGEAN'S CHURCH, ARBROATH NO6443

St Vigean's, Arbroath

Dedicated to St Vigean (or Fechin), Irish saint, died 664. Church rebuilt in 12th century, but not dedicated until 1242. Some 15th-century alterations. 19th-century restoration with lovely stained glass windows. Largely unaltered since. Sunday Service 11.30am

KEY AVAILABLE FROM HOUSE OPPOSITE CHURCH MAIN GATE

St Vigean's Museum also open

Church of Scotland **A**

St Vigean's Church, Arbroath

32 BRECHIN CATHEDRAL

Church Lane, Brechin

Founded in the 11th century, the round tower of that date is of Irish inspiration. 13th, 14th and 15th-century medieval architecture underwent major restoration in 1900–02 supervised by J. Honeyman (Honeyman, Keppie & Mackintosh). Special features include the 12th-century font and a collection of Pictish sculptures. Stunning 20th-century stained glass by Henry Holiday, Gordon Webster, Douglas Strachan, Herbert Hendrie, William Gauld, Hugh Easton and the firm of William Morris. The cathedral also contains the largest group of William Wilson windows in Scotland. Sunday Service 9am (with Holy Communion on 1st Sunday of month), 11am, 6.30pm (1st Sunday of month)

OPEN MOST DAYS ALL YEAR 9AM–4PM (GUIDES IN SUMMER MONTHS ONLY)

Afternoon teas in church hall, alternate Thursdays 2pm. Brechin Caledonian Railway nearby. Historical artefacts in Brechin Library

Church of Scotland WC **A**

33 LOWSON MEMORIAL CHURCH, FORFAR NO4350

Jameson Street, Forfar

A gem of a church, designed by A. Marshall Mackenzie, 1914. In the style of late Scots Gothic, cruciform in shape with 5-bay nave, aisleless transepts and a one-bay chancel. Built of a ruddy-hued local stone. Low central tower and squat spire. Wooden waggon roof. Excellent stained glass, Douglas Strachan. At east end of Forfar off Montrose Road. Sunday Service 11am also last Sunday 6.30pm

OPEN MONDAY TO FRIDAY 9.30AM–4.30PM ALL YEAR

Church of Scotland **A**

34 ST JOHN THE EVANGELIST, FORFAR

East High Street, Forfar

Built on the site of an earlier church, the present building was designed in Early English style by Sir R. Rowand Anderson and consecrated in 1881. The broach spire intended for the tower was never built. Panelling and redecoration of the roof by Sir Matthew Ochterlony, late 1940s. Altered in 1975 by Dr F.R. Stevenson to provide Lady Chapel and vestries. The font has traditionally been associated with St Margaret and Restenneth Priory. 3-manual pipe organ by Conacher of Huddersfield. Stained glass by Charles E. Kempe and Septimus Waugh. Queen Elizabeth The Queen Mother was confirmed in the church. Historic graveyard predates present church. Sunday Services 8.30 & 11am, weekdays as announced

OPEN DAILY SUMMER MONTHS 9AM–4PM, WINTER MONTHS 9AM–2PM

Scottish Episcopal **B**

35 GLEN PROSEN CHURCH

Glen Prosen, Kirriemuir

Present church built 1802, paid for by local inhabitants, ensuring continuous worship in the glen for nearly 400 years. Special features include wood carvings by Sir Robert Lorimer and War Memorial porch with rare slated cross. Sunday Service 2nd and 4th Sundays 12.15pm. Summer months Holy Communion (Scottish Episcopal) 4th Sunday, 8.30am. Songs of Praise for Guide Dogs for the Blind April–September 1st Sunday of month 6pm

OPEN DAILY, ACCESS VIA VESTRY DOOR

Teas available from Old School Restaurant, 400 yards, April–September

Church of Scotland **B**

Glen Prosen Church, Kirriemuir

36 KETTINS PARISH CHURCH

Kettins, by Coupar Angus

On the site of one of six chapels established by a nearby Columban monastery, the present church dates from 1768, with the north wing added in 1870 and the tower in 1891. 16 stained glass windows dating from 1878 onwards. Belgian bell of 1519 now rests, complete with belfry, close to the west gable it once surmounted. Celtic stone. Off A923, Dundee–Coupar Angus, 1¼ miles south-east of Coupar. Linked with Meigle. Sunday Service 11.30am

OPEN JUNE–AUGUST 1ST SUNDAY 2PM–4PM

Church of Scotland **B**

37 KIRRIEMUIR OLD PARISH CHURCH

Bank Street, Kirriemuir

9th-century stones were found when the church was rebuilt on this earlier Christian site in 1788 to a design by James Playfair, father of William Henry Playfair. The steeple was completed in 1790. Stained glass includes the triple window of The Last Supper, a Violet Jacobs window, and windows by William Wilson. Interesting kirkyard, the earliest stone dating from 1613. In centre of the town, behind Bank Street's shops. Sunday Service 9am and 11am

OPEN JUNE–AUGUST DAILY 10AM–12 NOON, 2–4PM

Church of Scotland **B**

38 ST MARY'S CHURCH, KIRRIEMUIR

NO384544

West Hillbank, Kirriemuir

Gothic revival church by Sir Ninian Comper, 1903 built to replace classical church of 1797 destroyed by fire. Stained glass by Comper and William Wilson. 2-manual tracker organ, Hamilton of Edinburgh, 1906. Sanctus bell, 1741. Conspicuous red sandstone bell tower. Sign posted to north side of the town. Sunday Services 9.30am Said Eucharist, 11am Sung Eucharist (except 4th Sunday Matins)

OPEN DAILY 10AM–4PM

Otherwise, key at Rectory, 128 Glengate, Kirriemuir

Scottish Episcopal **A**

St Mary's Church, Kirriemuir

39 ST MARGARET'S CHURCH, LUNANHEAD

Carsebarracks, Lunanhead

Built in the planned village of Carsebarracks on the site of an earlier chapel in 1907 by the builder/architect William L. McLean of Forfar as a gift of Mrs Susan Helen Gray of Bankhead House in memory of her husband. Stained glass window of the Crucifixion, 1913, by A.D. Fleming of London. 1909 mural by Miss W.M. Watson of Edinburgh. On the B9134 1 mile east of Forfar. Service 1st and 3rd Sundays excluding July and August 2pm

OPEN BY ARRANGEMENT

Contact Mr Orrock tel 01307 468156

Scottish Episcopal

40 HOLY TRINITY CHURCH, MONIFIETH NO4932

High Street, Monifieth

Black and white half-timbered style building by Mills & Shepherd, 1909. Originally intended as church hall, adapted to church. Pleasant sheltered garden. Buses from Dundee to Monifieth, Carnoustie and Arbroath stop outside. Sunday Services 8am, 10.30am, 6.30pm

OPEN DAILY

Scottish Episcopal WC B

Holy Trinity Church, Monifieth

41 MONTROSE OLD CHURCH NO7157

High Street, Montrose

1793 by John Gibson with a 'lovely flying-buttressed spire (J. Gillespie Graham, 1832) which is Montrose's town-mark' (Colin McWilliam, *Scottish Townscape*). By rail Intercity London to Aberdeen. Sunday Service 11am, also last Sunday 6.30pm

OPEN JUNE–AUGUST MONDAY TO FRIDAY 2PM–4.30PM

Church of Scotland A

· Argyll & Bute ·

42 ST JAMES' CHURCH, ARDBRECKNISH

Ardbrecknish

Built 1891, stone interior with fine series of monuments and excellent windows. Bells rehung, 1991. Grass churchyard overlooking Loch Awe. Sunday Service in summer 11am. Linked with St John's Cathedral, Oban

OPEN DAYLIGHT HOURS IN SUMMER

Scottish Episcopal

43 CHURCH OF THE HOLY SPIRIT, ARDCHATTAN

Ardchattan

Built 1886. Fine first world war memorial incorporating the 3 banners of Scotland, England and Ireland. Ardchattan crucifix on south wall. Stone pedestal font and ancient stone stoup. 1 mile west of Bonawe Quarry, beside Loch Etive. Sunday Service 2nd Sunday times vary. Linked with St John's Cathedral, Oban

OPEN BY ARRANGEMENT

Contact Mrs Colquhoun, The Ferry House, Ardchattan

Scottish Episcopal

44 KILMENY PARISH CHURCH, BALLYGRANT

Ballygrant, Isle of Islay

Kilmeny Parish Church is situated in sheltered wooded grounds. The present church was remodelled in the 1820s to plans by Thomas Telford on the site of the original church of 1790. There is evidence of a number of early Celtic Church foundations within the parish boundary, and nearby is the Finlaggan site, administrative centre of the Lords of the Isles. The church has received lovely gifts, most recently a new organ, gifted by the Caol Ila Distillery Company on the occasion of their 125th anniversary in 1996. Linked with Kilarrow. Situated above the main Port Askaig/Bowmore road. Sunday Service 12.30pm

OPEN JULY–AUGUST THURSDAY 10.30AM–12.30PM AND 2–4PM

Church of Scotland B

45 KILBRANDON KIRK, BALVICAR NM7616

Isle of Seil

Kilbrandon Kirk was built in 1866 and contains a beautiful set of five stained glass windows – the work of Douglas Strachan. The windows were commissioned by Miss Mackinnon of Ardmaddy Castle in 1937 in memory of her friend the Marchioness of Breadalbane. On the B8003, 1 mile south of the Balvicar turn-off. Sunday Service 10am, except last Sunday 11am

OPEN ALL YEAR

Church of Scotland (two steps) C

46 KILARROW PARISH CHURCH, BOWMORE

Bowmore, Isle of Islay

This 18th-century church, known as 'The Round Church', was built by Daniel Campbell of Shawfield and Islay in 1767. A year after the building commenced, the village of Bowmore came into being as a 'planned village' to rehouse those of the village of Kilarrow who were not directly involved in the work of Islay Estate, mainly agricultural workers and weavers. The 2-storey circular body of the church has a main central pillar 19 inches in diameter, possibly of hemlock oak, harled and plastered. Above the coved ceiling is a radial king-post roof truss into which eight major beams are jointed. The gallery was added in 1830, increasing its capacity to 500. Extensive renovation has been carried out in recent years. At the top of Main Street. Linked with Kilmeny. Sunday Service 11am

OPEN DAILY ALL YEAR 9AM–6PM

Church of Scotland A

47 HIGHLAND PARISH CHURCH, CAMPBELTOWN

New Quay Street, Campbeltown

"To be causewayed with whinstone and paved with hewn flags. The lock on the front door to be of 20/– value and the rest to have snecks and wooden bolts": the instruction of the architect George Dempster of Greenock, for a new church, built for the Highland, Gaelic-speaking, congregation of the area, and completed in 1807. Harled rubble with red sandstone dressings, an oblong with rectangular stair towers at each end of the front. Three galleries. The planned belfry was not large enough for the heritors, so a steeple was built; twice since it has been rebuilt, the casualty of lightning strikes. The pipe organ, Harrison & Harrison, Durham 1954, is a memorial to the fallen of World War II. Sunday Service 11.15am and 6.30pm

OPEN DAILY

Church of Scotland B

48 LORNE AND LOWLAND CHURCH, CAMPBELTOWN NR7120

Longrow, Campbeltown

Built in 1872 to the design of John Burnet, historically called The Longrow Church. Classical, influenced by Italian Renaissance style. Its bell tower is a well known landmark. Two stairways lead from the entrance foyer to a horse-shoe gallery. Fine plaster ceiling. Pulpit 1895. Sunday Services 11.15am, 7pm (fortnightly)

OPEN JULY–AUGUST MONDAY TO FRIDAY 11AM–4PM

Other times contact Mr J. Gill tel 01586 552781

Church of Scotland C

49 CARDROSS PARISH CHURCH NS3477

Station Road, Cardross

Church founded 1225 on west bank of River Leven and rebuilt in village, 1640. Present building 1872. Stained glass windows, Sadie McLennan 1972, embroidered panels, Hannah Frew Paterson 1981, woven silk hangings, Sarah Sumsion 1990, and engraved glass windows, John Lawrie 1992. Peal of six bells. A82 from Glasgow; half hourly train service from Glasgow Queen Street. Sunday Services 9.30am & 11am, June, July, August 11am only, also September to Easter 2nd Sunday 7pm

OPEN MONDAY, WEDNESDAY, FRIDAY MORNINGS

Or by arrangement, contact Mrs S. McLatchie, tel 01389 841509

Church of Scotland B

Cardross Parish Church

50 COLINTRAIVE CHURCH NS0374

Colintraive

Erected 1840 by Mrs Campbell of Southhall as a chapel of ease, part of Inverchaolain Parish. Became a Free Church in 1843, United Free in 1900 and returned to the Church of Scotland in 1929. United with Kilmodan Church. Spectacular views over Kyles of Bute. Sunday Service 10am or 11.30am alternating monthly with Kilmodan

OPEN DAILY

Church of Scotland

51 ST ORAN'S CHURCH, CONNEL NM9134

Gothic Revival cruciform church of 1888 with lancet and pointed traceried windows, gabled porch and a central tower with corbelled parapet. Good interior with open timbered ceiling. 20th-century glass by various artists. Beautiful views up Loch Etive from garden. On A85. Sunday Service 11am

OPEN DURING DAYLIGHT HOURS

Church of Scotland B

52 DUNOON BAPTIST CHURCH CENTRE NS1776

9 Alexandra Parade, Dunoon

Formerly the American servicemen's YMCA. The centre welcomes all visitors to the beautiful Cowal Peninsula. Browse in the well stocked Christian book and gift shop. Sample excellent coffee and home baking with a splendid view of the Clyde estuary. Next to Tourist Information Centre and five minutes from the pier. Sunday Services 11am & 6.30pm

OPEN MONDAY TO SATURDAY 10AM–4PM

Baptist (church) A

53 DUNOON OLD AND ST CUTHBERT'S CHURCH

Church Square, Dunoon

The present building probably stands on the site of a much earlier church which until 1688 was the Cathedral Church of both the Roman Catholic and Episcopalian Bishops of Argyll. Towards the end of the 18th century the building became dilapidated and was demolished, the stone being used to build Gillespie Graham's Late Decorated Gothic Revival church of 1816. The belfry tower was added in 1839 and the church was lengthened and widened by Andrew Balfour in 1909. Chancel window, 1939 by Douglas Hamilton. Gravestones of the 13th and 17th century in the kirkyard. Sunday Service 11am

OPEN BY ARRANGEMENT

Contact the Revd P. Lang, 1 Royal Crescent, Dunoon tel 01369 701291

Church of Scotland WC B

54 ST JOHN'S CHURCH, DUNOON

Argyll Street, Dunoon

A magnificent nave and aisles kirk by R.A. Bryden, 1877, built to supersede the original Free Church of 1843. Normandy Gothic spired tower. Galleried 'concert hall' interior. Raised choir behind central pulpit. 3-manual pipe organ by Brook & Co., 1895. Interesting stained glass including windows by Stephen Adam and Gordon Webster, also Lauder Memorial. Sunday Services 10.15am & 6.30pm

OPEN JUNE, JULY & AUGUST MONDAY TO FRIDAY 10AM–12 NOON, 2–4PM

4th St John's Music Festival 1998 September Sundays at 3pm, information tel 01369 830639

Church of Scotland WC B

55 GIGHA AND CARA PARISH CHURCH

Isle of Gigha

Built 1923. Windows by Gordon Webster. First minister Dr Kenneth MacLeod author of 'The Road to the Isles'. Gigha Gardens and 9–hole golf course 10 minutes walk from church. Ferry from Tayinloan/Kintyre 20 minutes. Sunday Service 12 noon

OPEN DAILY

Church of Scotland WC at village shop

56 GLENARAY & INVERARAY PARISH CHURCH NN0908

Church Square, Inveraray

Designed by Robert Mylne in 1792 to house two congregations, English and Gaelic. A solid wall separated the two. Gaelic portion converted to church hall, 1957. Sunday Service 11.15am

OPEN APRIL–OCTOBER DAILY 9AM–5PM

Church of Scotland **A**

Glenaray & Inveraray Parish Church

57 KILMODAN CHURCH, GLENDARUEL NR9983

Clachan of Glendaruel

A Georgian T-plan church of 1783 on site of an earlier church of 1610. Completely restored in 1983. Segmental-arched windows; lofts in the three arms. Two long narrow communion tables. Memorial to Revd John MacLaurin and his two famous sons (Colin, author of MacLaurin's Mathematical Theorem). Bus and post bus from Dunoon. On A886. United with Colintraive. Sunday Services 10am or 11.30am alternating monthly with Colintraive

OPEN DAILY

Church of Scotland wc (nearby)

58 ST MICHAEL AND ALL ANGELS, HELENSBURGH NS2982

William Street, Helensburgh

Built by Robert Rowand Anderson in 1868 in French Gothic style. The tower, with its peal of eight bells, was added in 1930 and the porch in 1996. Richly decorated interior, with acanthus-leaf capitals to the columns and St Michael in the centre of the carved oak porch screen. The pipe organ is by August Gern. 800m west of Central railway station, off Clyde Street. Services Sunday 8am, 10.15am & 6.30pm, Tuesdays 10.30am, Wednesdays 7.30pm

OPEN DAILY 9AM–5PM

Scottish Episcopal wc **A**

59 THE WEST KIRK OF HELENSBURGH

Colquhoun Square, Helensburgh

Victorian Gothic building of 1853, J., W.H. & J.M. Hay, restored after disastrous fire in 1924 by Robert Wemyss, with a porch by William Leiper. Impressive panelled interior, with fine woodwork and half-timbered ceiling. Exceptionally fine stained glass including memorial windows to Andrew Bonar Law, one time Prime Minister, and to John Logie Baird, inventor of televison and son of the Manse in Helensburgh. Hill House (C. Rennie Mackintosh) is 1 mile away. Sunday Service 10am April–September 11am October–March

OPEN DAILY ALL YEAR 9AM–5PM, AND WITH GUIDES JUNE–AUGUST MONDAY, WEDNESDAY & FRIDAY 2–4PM

Church of Scotland wc **B**

60 IONA ABBEY

Isle of Iona

On the original site of St Columba's monastery *c* 563AD. St Columba's Shrine dates from the 9th century, most of the present buildings from around 1200. The massive restoration of the Abbey Church was undertaken by the Iona Cathedral Trust, who own and care for the buildings, and was completed in 1910. The Iona Community now occupy the monastic buildings which they restored under the leadership of the Revd Dr George MacLeod. Beautiful Augustinian nunnery, 12th-century ruin, Reilig Odhrain (Royal burial ground), 'Street of the Dead', imposing standing crosses and one of the largest collections of early Christian carved stones in Europe. Ferry from Oban to Mull, by bus/car to Fionnphort, pedestrian ferry to Iona. Sunday Service March–October 10.30am Monday to Saturday 9am all year

OPEN AT ALL TIMES

Inter-denominational ☐ ⚱ ⬔ ☐ ☕ wc **A**

61 IONA PARISH CHURCH

Isle of Iona

A Thomas Telford church of 1828. Pews, pulpit and communion table realigned in 1939. Former manse of same date now a heritage centre with picnic area adjacent. Ferry from Oban to Mull. Bus/car to Fionnphort for ferry to Iona. Sunday Service 12 noon. Short Service Tuesday 1pm and each weekday in high summer

OPEN DAILY

Church of Scotland **B**

Iona Parish Church

62 KILBERRY PARISH CHURCH NR7164

The church was built in 1821. A plain oblong building, galleries on three sides, later alterations provided an internal stair and removed the original external access. At Lergnahension, 12 miles from Tarbert on the B8024. Sunday Services fortnightly, summer 10am, winter 2pm

OPEN ALL YEAR DURING DAYLIGHT HOURS

Church of Scotland ⬔ **B**

63 KILFINAN PARISH CHURCH NR9378

Kilfinan, North Knapdale

A place of worship since 1235. 1759 Gothic, including the earlier Lamont Vault of 1633. Stones of interest. B8000 from Tighnabruaich or Strachur. Sunday Service 12 noon

OPEN ALL YEAR

Church of Scotland **B**

64 KILMARTIN PARISH CHURCH

NR8398

Kilfinan, North Knapdale

On the site of earlier churches, the present building opened in 1835. The architect was James Gordon Davis. Three interesting memorial panels from the 18th and 19th-centuries to members of the family of Campbell of Duntroon. The church has two outstanding crosses, with explanatory panels provided by Historic Scotland. The kirkyard contains the mausoleum of Bishop Neil Campbell and medieval tomb slabs. Extensive views over Bronze Age burial cairns. For Services see local paper and notice board

OPEN APRIL–OCTOBER 9.30AM–6PM

Church of Scotland B

Kilmartin Parish Church

65 KILMUN PARISH CHURCH, ST MUNN'S

NS1781

Kilmun, By Dunoon

On the site of a 7th-century Celtic monastery, overlooking Holy Loch. Tower of 15th-century collegiate church. Present building dates from 1841, by Thomas Burns with interior remodelled by P. MacGregor Chalmers in 1899. Important stained glass by Stephen Adam and Alfred Webster. Water-powered organ. Ancient graveyard with fine 18th-century carved stones. Mausoleum of Dukes of Argyll, Douglas vault. Grave of Elizabeth Blackwell, first lady doctor. On A880, 6 miles from Dunoon. Sunday Service 12 noon

OPEN MAY–SEPTEMBER TUESDAY–THURSDAY 1.30–4.30PM (LAST TOUR 4PM)

Other times, including weekends and holidays, and coach parties any time, by arrangement

Contact Valerie Gillies tel 01369 840342

Younger Botanic Gardens 2 miles, open April–October

Church of Scotland WC B

66 ST FINAN'S CHURCH, KINLOCHMOIDART

The church stands on a ledge of level ground in woodland above the mouth of the River Moidart and below an impressively steep hillside. It was built in 1857, to a design by Alexander Ross, in simple Early English style, with crow-stepped gables, a small belfry and a porch. There are two unusual stained glass windows by the Victorian artist Jemima Blackburn. Up a track leading off the A861 ½ mile north of the bridge over the River Moidart. Sunday Service Easter and May–September 5.30pm

OPEN DAILY

Scottish Episcopal C

67 KIEL CHURCH, LOCHALINE

Lochaline, Morvern

The present church is the third on this site. Ruins of a medieval church are on the site of the original and much earlier building which, according to legend, was erected at the command of St Columba. Today's church was designed by P. MacGregor Chalmers, 1898. Interesting stained glass. Memorial plaque to the MacLeods, father and son, whose ministry here spanned more than a century. 15th-century cross outside the front of the church. The nearby 18th-century Session House contains a collection of carved stones 8th to 16th-centuries. 1 mile out of the village on the Drimnin road. Sunday Service 11am

OPEN DAILY ALL YEAR

Special centenary events in 1998. Contact the Minister tel 01967 421267

Church of Scotland **C**

68 LOCHGOILHEAD & KILMORICH PARISH CHURCH NN2001

Lochgoilhead

Dedicated to the Three Holy Brethren, the church is first mentioned in Papal letters of 1379. It was rebuilt in the 18th century incorporating the medieval walls. Many features of interest. A83 Arrochar–Inveraray, Top of Rest and Be Thankful, B828 & B839 into village. Sunday Service 10.30am

OPEN BY ARRANGEMENT

Contact Mr W. Workman tel 013013 280

Church Fair in August. Coffee mornings depending on local weather conditions

Church of Scotland **B**

69 LUSS PARISH CHURCH NS3692

This picturesque church, the third built on this site on the banks of Loch Lomond, with its beautiful stained glass windows and uniquely timbered roof, features frequently in 'Take the High Road'. The ancient graveyard has 15 listed ancient monuments. Luss Village, off A82. Sunday Service 11.45am

OPEN DAILY FROM 10AM

Church of Scotland **B**

70 CATHEDRAL CHURCH OF ST JOHN THE DIVINE, OBAN NM8629

George Street, Oban

The cathedral is a small part of the projected building, consisting of chancel, crossing, nave of one bay and one transept, James Chalmers, 1908, attached at right angles to existing church by Charles Wilson and David Thomson, giving an extraordinary building internally. Tall reredos on a Scottish theme with painting of Ascension set in the West Highlands by Norman Macdougall. Vast hovering bronze eagle. Choir stalls in form of Celtic graveyard. Much Iona marble and terrazzo. Sunday Services 8am, 10.15am, 11.30am & 5pm. Weekdays 9.30am or 11am

OPEN DAILY

Scottish Episcopal WC **C**

71 TARBERT PARISH CHURCH NR8668

Campbeltown Road, Tarbert

Built in 1886 on the site of an earlier mission church dating from 1775 and granted *quoad sacra* status in 1864. Architects J. McKissack and W.G. Rowan of Glasgow. The building features an imposing square tower rising over 100 feet, surmounted by a crown and lantern. Stained glass windows and unusual roof decoration. 18th-century graveyard within walking distance. Sunday Service 11.30am

OPEN APRIL–SEPTEMBER 10AM–5.30PM

Church of Scotland B

Tarbert Parish Church

72 KILCHATTAN KIRK, TOBERONOCHY NM7408

Isle of Luing

Kilchattan Kirk was built in 1936 and houses a beautifully carved, floor-standing, wooden lectern and two wooden offering plates donated by Latvian ship owners to mark the rescue efforts of the islanders when one of their ships foundered in a storm on the island of Belnahua in 1938. Just beyond the school on the road to Toberonochy. Sunday Service 11am, except last Sunday in month 3.15pm

OPEN ALL YEAR

Church of Scotland

· East Ayrshire ·

73 CATRINE PARISH CHURCH NS5225

Chapel Brae, Catrine

Charming church, built as a chapel of ease in 1792, financed by Sir Claud Alexander of Ballochmyle. It was established as a parish church when Catrine was made a *quoad sacra* parish in 1871. Major renovations in 1874, 1960 and 1992. Stained glass. Harrison & Harrison pipe organ, 1874. Overlooking Catrine in the river Ayr valley. B713, off A76 Dumfries–Kilmarnock, between Mauchline and Auchinleck. Sunday Service 12 noon

OPEN BY ARRANGEMENT

Contact Mr Holland tel 01290 5515718

Church of Scotland WC A

74 GALSTON PARISH CHURCH (ST PETER'S) NS5036

Cross Street, Galston

Built 1809, John Brash, Glasgow, on a site of Christian worship since 1252. Chancel added 1912. 3-manual pipe organ, J.J. Binns, 1913. The Revd Robert Stirling, Minister 1824–78, was the inventor of the Stirling steam engine. Covenanters' graves and memorial. Junction of A719 with A71. Sunday Service 11am

OPEN AUGUST 8TH & 9TH, FLOWER FESTIVAL AND RESTORATION FUND EVENTS

Other times contact Mrs McHoull tel 01563 820890

Church of Scotland ♿ ② ⚱ wc **B**

75 HENDERSON PARISH CHURCH, KILMARNOCK NS4237

London Road, Kilmarnock

Brilliantly individual Arts & Crafts treatment of Gothic motifs by Thomas Smellie, Kilmarnock, completed in 1907. Very tall tower above tall church built on rising ground, with halls below. Carillon of bells, 1950. Fine Norman & Beard 3-manual organ restored in 1987. Stained glass windows by Gordon Webster, 1907, and, in side chapel, by Wendy Robertson, 1987. On Burns Heritage Trail, leading to Dean Castle Country Park (open all year). Church in town centre, adjacent to Grand Hall, Palace Theatre and bus station. Sunday Services 9.45am & 11am

OPEN BY ARRANGEMENT

Contact Mr J. Neil tel 01563 528212

Church of Scotland ♿ ② ☐ ⚱ 🗄 ☕ wc **B**

76 HOLY TRINITY CHURCH, KILMARNOCK

Portland Road, Kilmarnock

The nave to a design by James Wallace, 1857, with chancel and sanctuary by Sir George Gilbert Scott, 1876. Wall and ceiling murals in the chancel, stained glass. At the junction of Portland Road with Dundonald Road, 200 yards from King Street. Sunday Services 9.15am Holy Communion, 11am Sung Eucharist, 6pm Evensong. Matins 11am 1st Sunday if not a festival

OPEN DAILY

Scottish Episcopal ② 🗄 **B**

Holy Trinity Church, Kilmarnock

77 LAIGH KIRK, KILMARNOCK

John Dickie Street, Kilmarnock

Body of the church by Robert Johnstone, 1802. Enlarged 1831 with later 19th-century session room. Major refurbishment, 1996 by W.I. Munro Architects, winning 1997 Civic Trust Award for part of town centre regeneration. Interesting monuments and stained glass. Covenanters' graves in adjacent kirkyard. Close to bus and rail stations. Sunday Services 11am also 9.30am June–August

OPEN TUESDAY, THURSDAY AND FRIDAY MORNING

Other times tel 01563 524040

Church of Scotland 🦽 ⑦ 🗂 ⛪ 🚻 **A**

78 ST MARNOCK'S PARISH CHURCH, KILMARNOCK

St Marnock's Street, Kilmarnock

Perpendicular Gothic, rectangular plan 6-bay church with centrally placed tower on north gable end, by John Ingram, 1839. Fine carillon of bells. 3-manual pipe organ, 1872, painted organ screen. Extensive restoration programme completed in 1997. In centre of town with easy access from bus and railway station. Sunday Services 11am

OPEN SUNDAY 6 SEPTEMBER 12 NOON–4PM

Or by arrangement contact the Session Clerk tel 01563 523951

Church of Scotland ⑦ ⛪ 🗂 🍵 🚻 **B**

79 ST MAUR'S GLENCAIRN PARISH CHURCH, KILMAURS

The church at Kilmaurs was in the possession of Kelso Abbey as early as 1170. In 1413 the present foundation was endowed by Sir William Cunninghame as a collegiate church. Rebuilt by Robert S. Ingram,1888, in a cruciform shape. 20th-century stained glass, including a window by Roland Mitton of Livingston, and three rose windows. The clock tower holds the original bell inscribed 'Michael Burgerhuys Me Fecit 1618'. Glencairn Aisle adjacent to the church with sculptured mural, 1600, commissioned by James 7th Earl of Glencairn, in memory of the Earl and Countess of Glencairn, and worked by David Scougal, mason and burgess. On A735. Sunday Service 11am

OPEN BY ARRANGEMENT

Contact the Revd John Urquhart tel 01563 538289

Church of Scotland 🦽 ⑦ **B**

80 MAUCHLINE PARISH CHURCH NS4927

Loudoun Street, Mauchline

Present church, by William Alexander, 1829, stands on site of St Michael's Church founded in 13th century. Single bell cast in 1742. Willis pipe organ, 1888, rebuilt in 1980. Associations with covenanters and Robert Burns, many of whose contemporaries are buried here. At junction of B743 with A76. Sunday Service 11am

OPEN JUNE–AUGUST TUESDAY & WEDNESDAY 2–4PM

Also Ayrshire Doors Open Day – date to be announced

Church of Scotland 🦽 ☐ ⛪ 🗂 ⑦ 🚻 **B**

81 SORN PARISH CHURCH NS5526

Main Street, Sorn

A rather splendid edifice, quietly assured, built in 1656 and much reconstructed in 1826. Outside stairs to three galleries. Jougs on the west wall. East wall memorial to George Wood, last covenanter to die, 1688. Sunday Service 10.30am

OPEN BY ARRANGEMENT

Contact Miss McKerrow tel 01290 551256

Church of Scotland WC B

Sorn Parish Church

82 ST COLUMBA'S PARISH CHURCH, STEWARTON NS4245

1 Kirk Glebe, Stewarton

Built in 1696, renovated in 1775 and widened in 1825 with later additions. Bell tower. Lainshaw Loft used for smaller services. New and restored windows installed for tercentenary in 1996. Beside the mini-roundabout at the south end of Stewarton. Sunday Service 11am

OPEN BY ARRANGEMENT

Contact the Minister tel 01560 482453

Church of Scotland WC B

St Columba's Parish Church, Stewarton

· North Ayrshire ·

83 BEITH HIGH CHURCH NS3553

Kirk Road, Beith

Built in 1807 and extended in 1885. Gothic T-plan kirk dominated by the tall 5-stage tower. Stained glass by Gordon Webster. Harrison & Harrison pipe organ, 1885. From Beith bypass along Barrmill Road to Kirk Road. Sunday Services 10 & 11.30am

OPEN BY ARRANGEMENT

Contact Mr Alex Sanderson at Church Hall tel 01505 502104

Church of Scotland WC B

84 THE CATHEDRAL OF THE ISLES, CUMBRAE NS1654

College Street, Millport, Isle of Cumbrae

Cathedral, college and cloister by William Butterfield, 1851. A Tractarian church built by 6th Earl of Glasgow. Peal of bells, organ, stained glass by William Wailes and Hardman. Visitors welcome to picnic in the grounds. Ferry from Largs and bus to Millport. Sunday Service 11am Sung Eucharist, other times see notice board in porch

OPEN DAILY

Scottish Episcopal WC A

85 ST MARGARET'S PARISH CHURCH, DALRY NS2949

The Cross, Dalry

1873, a 'powerful, carefully handled composition' by David Thomson, on the site of an earlier church of 1604. Dedicated to St Margaret of Antioch. Major restoration after fire in 1950s gives an interior of deep solemnity enhanced by good glass by Webster, Payne, Moody, Guthrie & Wells, including an amount of rare Munich glass. Hemony bell, 1661 only example in UK church. 159-ft floodlit spire. A737 to Dalry, in centre. Sunday Services 10.30 & 11.30am, June–August, 11.30am & 6.30pm September–May

OPEN BY ARRANGEMENT

Also Ayrshire Doors Open Day tel 01294 833135 or 832234

Church of Scotland WC B

86 ST ANDREW'S PARISH CHURCH (FERGUSON MEMORIAL), IRVINE

Caldon Road x Oaklands Avenue, Irvine

St Andrew's was gifted in 1957 to commemorate the centenary of the death of John Ferguson, founder of the Ferguson bequest. The congregation has shared the church with the local Scottish Episcopalian congregation who built on a chapel/meeting room and coffee lounge in 1981. Sunday Services Scottish Episcopal 9.30am, Church of Scotland 11.15am

OPEN TUESDAYS 10–10.45AM

Tuesday Morning Club for Senior Citizens with tea and coffee in coffee lounge

Church of Scotland WC

87 THE AULD KIRK OF KILBIRNIE

Dalry Road, Kilbirnie

A pre-Reformation church on or near the site of 6th-century Christian settlement of St Brendan of Clonfert. The nave dates from 1470 and the tower from 1490. Glengarnock aisle added 1597. Crawfurd aisle with Laird's loft and splendid Italian Renaissance-style carving 1642. Pulpit *c* 1620. Signed from B737 Irvine–Paisley. By bus to Kilbirnie, by rail to Glengarnock. Sunday Service September–May 11am & 6.30pm, June–August 9.30am & 11am

OPEN JULY–AUGUST WEEKDAYS 2–4PM & AYRSHIRE DOORS OPEN DAY SEPTEMBER

Other times contact Mr J. Lauchland tel 01505 683459

Church of Scotland A

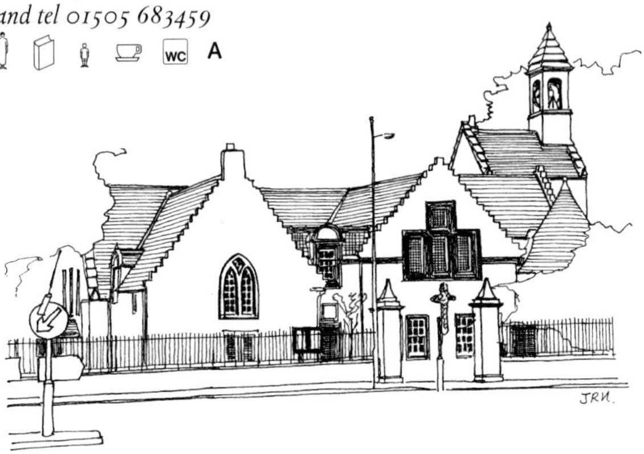

The Auld Kirk of Kilbirnie

88 THE ABBEY CHURCH, KILWINNING

NS3043

Main Street, Kilwinning

Built in 1774 by John Garland and John Wright. The church is on the site of the ruined Abbey, founded in 1188, and replaced a second church of 1590. Visitor Centre in Abbey tower. Abbey ruins. Sunday Services 9.15am & 11am September–June, 10am July and August

OPEN AYRSHIRE DOORS OPEN DAY AND BY ARRANGEMENT

Contact Mr J. Muir 30 Underwood, Kilwinning tel 01294 552929

Church of Scotland

89 LAMLASH PARISH CHURCH

Shore Road, Lamlash, Isle of Arran

A massive campanile tower over 90-ft high sits above this Gothic-style, red sandstone building by H. & D. Barclay, 1886. The church was built by 12th Duke of Hamilton to replace an earlier building of 1773. Boarded, barrel-vaulted ceiling and carved, wooden tripartite Gothic sedilia. Seven stained glass windows by Meiklejohn, Gordon Webster and Christian Shaw; all other windows are hand painted, German cathedral glass. Pipe organ, William Hill, Norman and Beard, 1934. In the front grounds are an ancient cross and baptismal font from the old monastery on Holy Isle in Lamlash Bay. Major restoration programme begun 1997. Sunday Service 11.30am

OPEN BY ARRANGEMENT

See church notice board for information or contact Capt J.L. Davidson, Rock Cottage, Cordon, Lamlash tel 01770 600787

Church of Scotland A

90 CLARK MEMORIAL CHURCH, LARGS

Bath Street, Largs

Gifted by John Clark of the Anchor Thread Mills, Paisley, and designed by William Kerr of T.G. Abercrombie, Paisley 1892. Red sandstone from Locharbriggs and Corsehill in Early English Gothic style. Superb stained glass, all maufactured in Glasgow at height of Arts and Crafts movement. Hammer beam roof. Views of the Clyde and Cumbraes. Sunday Services 9.30 & 11am, Thursday 10.30am

OPEN BY ARRANGEMENT (NOT THURSDAYS)

Contact Church Officer tel 01475 675186

Viking Festival one week each September

Church of Scotland WC A

Clark Memorial Church, Largs

91 ST COLUMBA'S PARISH CHURCH, LARGS NS2059

Gallowgate, Largs

The old parish church was replaced by the present building in 1892. It is a handsome structure, architects Henry Steele and Andrew Balfour, of red stone with a 3-stage tower with spire and clock. Interesting carved octagonal oak pulpit and notable windows, "Father" Willis organ. Memorial to General Sir Thomas MacDougall Brisbane, astronomer & soldier & Governor of NSW. Sunday Service 11am

OPEN 10AM–NOON MONDAY–FRIDAY

Church of Scotland (by arrangement) (Saturdays June–September) WC B

92 ST CUTHBERT'S PARISH CHURCH, SALTCOATS

Caledonia Road, Saltcoats

Designed by Peter MacGregor Chalmers and dedicated in 1908, the fourth building of the congregation of Ardrossan Parish. The chancel displays a marble reredos of the Last Supper. Sixteen stained glass windows the Life of Christ by William Wilson, 1947; two windows by Gordon Webster, 1976. Model of a French frigate of 1804, by a sailor William Dunlop hangs in the church. He made it as a thanksgiving for his surviving the Napoleonic wars when a canonball narrowly missed his hammock! Sunday Service 11.15am

OPEN BY ARRANGEMENT

Contact Mrs Hanlon tel 01294 466636

Church of Scotland WC B

· South Ayrshire ·

93 ALLOWAY PARISH CHURCH NS3318

Alloway

Built in 1858, Campbell Douglas. South transept added in 1877, chancel built and nave extended in 1890. Excellent stained glass including Stephen Adam, Clayton & Bell, Gordon Webster, W. & J.J. Keir. Douglas McLundie's memorial window to D.F. McIntyre, pilot on first flight over Mount Everest in 1933. Two windows by Susan Bradbury were installed in 1996, one depicting the four seasons, the other in memory of Robert Burns. B7024 south of Burns' cottage. Sunday Services 9.45am & 11.15am

OPEN JUNE–SEPTEMBER MONDAY TO FRIDAY 10AM–4PM

Conducted tours contact local tourist office

Church of Scotland B

94 HOLY TRINITY CHURCH, AYR NS3321

Fullarton Street, Ayr

Dedicated in 1888. Scotland's major example of the work of J.L. Pearson, designer of Truro Cathedral. Pulpit of Caen stone and very fine stained glass windows by, among others, Clayton & Bell. Next to Ayr bus station, walking distance from railway station. Sunday Services 8am, 10.30am and 6.30pm, Wednesday Eucharist 11am

OPEN MORNINGS IN SUMMER

Concert series

Scottish Episcopal (for visiting groups by arrangement) WC A

95 BALLANTRAE PARISH CHURCH NX0882

Main Street, Ballantrae

Built in 1819. Memorial to Lord Ballantrae. Regency pulpit. Nephew of Robert Burns was Minister, 1826–30. Kennedy tomb beside church. Ruins of Ardstinchar Castle. A77. Railway station at Girvan, 13 miles. Buses from Glasgow. United with Glenapp. Sunday Service 11am

OPEN DAILY MAY–SEPTEMBER 10AM–SUNSET

Church of Scotland WC (in village) B

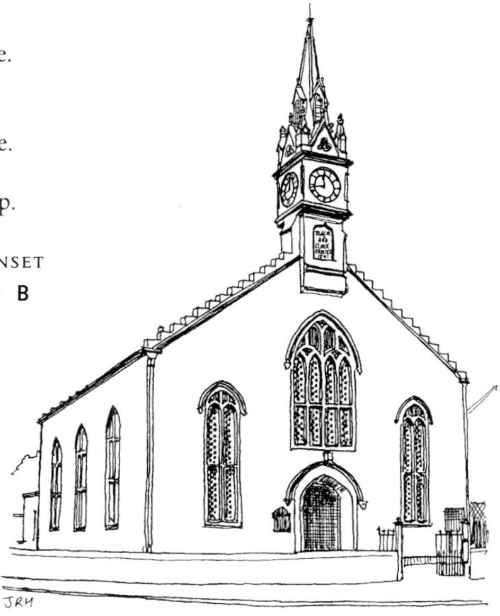

Ballantrae Parish Church

96 BARR PARISH CHURCH NX2794

Main Street, Barr, by Girvan

Dating from 1878, built to a design by A. Stevenson. Early Gothic gabled chapel. Slate roof, skew gables, rubble walls, freestone dressings. Picturesque south east bellcote. Fine wooden ceiling. Restored in 1978, P.J. Lorimer, London. B734 from Girvan. Occasional buses from Girvan. Sunday Service 12 noon

OPEN ALL YEAR 9AM–7PM

Teas July & August Monday, Friday & Saturday 2.30–5pm

Church of Scotland WC C

97 DUNDONALD PARISH CHURCH

Main Street, Dundonald

Tranquil setting for this traditional stone church of 1804, built on the site of an earlier building. The clock tower was added in 1841, and the chancel in 1906. Some fine stained glass, particularly Henry Dearle's unique 'Last Supper'. Pipe organ, Norman & Beard 1906. Interesting grave stones in the tidy graveyard. Sunday Service 11am

OPEN BY ARRANGEMENT

Contact Revd Robert Mayes tel 01563 850243

Church of Scotland WC B

98 SACRED HEARTS OF JESUS AND MARY, GIRVAN NX1897

Harbour Lane, Girvan

A plain Gothic structure of 1860 with a huge prow-like porch added in 1959 by Stevenson & Ferguson. Stained glass windows of 1860. Services 7pm Saturday and 9 & 11am Sunday

OPEN DURING DAYLIGHT HOURS

Roman Catholic

99 GLENAPP CHURCH

Glenapp

Memorial window to Elsie Mackay, 3rd daughter of Earl of Inchcape. She was killed in 1928 attempting to fly the Atlantic. Modern stained glass window above door, 'The Stilling of the Tempest', in memory of 1st Earl. Graveyard contains tombs of the three Earls of Inchcape. 7 miles south of Ballantrae on A77, 10 miles north of Stranraer. United with Ballantrae. Sunday Service occasional

OPEN SUMMER & AUTUMN

Church of Scotland

Kirkmichael Parish Church

100 KIRKMICHAEL PARISH CHURCH NS3408

80 Patna Road, Kirkmichael, near Maybole

Believed to stand on the site of a 13th-century church under the care of the monks of Whithorn, the present church was built in 1787 by Hugh Cairncross, and the belfry rebuilt in 1887. Stone pulpit of 1919 depicting St Michael, St George, St Andrew and St Patrick incorporates the war memorial. The oldest building is the lychgate, the bell inside is dated 1702 and is still rung when a bride leaves the church after her wedding. Interesting stones in surrounding graveyard including Covenanter's memorial. 2 miles east of Maybole. Sunday Service 10.30am

OPEN BY ARRANGEMENT

Contact the Minister tel 01655 750286

Church of Scotland (in village) WC **B**

101 KIRKOSWALD PARISH CHURCH NS2407

Robert Adam, 1777, contemporary with Culzean. It is suggested that Adam, touring with Lord Cassillis, his client at Culzean, came across the church during construction and recommended some changes, giving the building fine Palladian details. The church was visited by Robert Burns and President Eisenhower. Burns characters, Tam O'Shanter, Souter Johnnie and Kirkton Jean, are buried in the old graveyard. On the A77, 5 miles from Maybole. Sunday Service 11am

OPEN DURING DAYLIGHT HOURS

Church of Scotland **A**

102 STRAITON PARISH CHURCH (ST CUTHBERT'S) NS3804

The main part of the church dates from 1758. The piscina of the original church is still visible on the east wall. Chantry chapel of late 15th century containing various memorial plaques to members of the Hunter Blair family. In 1901 the church was renovated by John Kinross and the bell tower was added to the design of John Murdoch. The interior is noted for its beautiful carvings, especially on the ceiling and pulpit. Tapestry cushions, 1993, depict themes from the life and work of the community. The stone font is the gift of the Fergusson family. Splendid stained glass. Covenanter's memorial in graveyard. Straiton is 4 miles east of Kirkmichael. Sunday Service noon

OPEN BY ARRANGEMENT

Contact the Minister tel 01655 750286

Church of Scotland (in village) WC (nearby) **A**

Straiton Parish Church (St Cuthbert's)

103 OUR LADY AND ST MEDDAN CHURCH, TROON NS3230

4 Cessnock Road, Troon

Built to a design by Reginald Fairlie, 1910. 2 minutes from railway station, Glasgow–Ayr, half hourly train service. Sunday Mass 9 & 11.15am, Saturday Vigil Mass 6pm

OPEN DAILY UNTIL 4PM AND AYRSHIRE DOORS OPEN DAY SEPTEMBER

Roman Catholic A

104 PORTLAND PARISH CHURCH, TROON

St Meddan's Street, Troon

Opened in 1914 as a United Free Church. By H.E. Clifford & Lunan. Perpendicular Gothic in white sandstone with fine tracery on the great north window which is repeated in the nave windows. Interior has exposed stone with blonde Austrian oak pews and fittings. Harrison & Harrison 2-manual organ, rebuilt 1970. Halls extension added 1964. Two minutes walk from railway station. Sunday Service 9.30am and 11.15am

OPEN JULY & AUGUST TUESDAY AND THURSDAY 2–4.30PM

Church of Scotland (south beach entrance) WC B

· Borders ·

105 BEDRULE CHURCH NT6017

Bedrule, by Jedburgh

Beautifully rebuilt in 1914 by T. Greenshields Leadbetter, the church has a plaque commemorating Bishop Turnbull, founder of Glasgow University. Stained glass, including Woman's Guild centenary window, 1992 and windows by Douglas Strachan, 1922. Fine views over Rule Valley to Ruberslaw. Linked with Denholm and Minto. Sunday Service fortnightly alternating with Bedrule: February–May 11.30am, June–September 10am, October–January 11.30am

OPEN DURING DAYLIGHT HOURS

Joint opening with Denholm and Minto Saturday 27 June, Wednesdays 8 & 15 July, teas at the Manse, Leyden's Road, Denholm

Church of Scotland B

106 BOWDEN KIRK NT5530

Sitting by St Cuthbert's Way, the pilgrim route from Melrose to Lindisfarne, the church has a wealth of architectural history. It was founded in 1128, part of the north wall is possibly 15th-century, east end from 1644, cross aisle from 1661, west gable and doorway at west end of north wall 17th-century. Repaired in 1794 and with major alterations in 1909 by P. MacGregor Chalmers. Carved wooden 17th-century laird's loft for Riddell-Carre family. Burial vaults of Riddel-Carre of Cavers-Carre and Dukes of Roxburghe. Memorials, including one to Lady Grizell Baillie, first Deaconess of the Church of Scotland. Many notable tombstones in graveyard. Sunday Service 11am

OPEN DURING DAYLIGHT HOURS

Church of Scotland (from post office) WC A

107 BROUGHTON, GLENHOLM AND KILBUCHO PARISH CHURCH

Broughton, Biggar

Built in 1804 and extended by Robert Bryden of Broughton and Glasgow, 1886, to whom there is a memorial stained glass window in the north wall. Roof lights above the communion table are based on originals in Copenhagen Museum. Linked with Tweedsmuir, Skirling and Stobo with Drumelzier. Sunday Service 10.30am

OPEN BY ARRANGEMENT

Contact Mr Donald Strathairn tel 01899 830226

Church of Scotland

108 COLDSTREAM PARISH CHURCH

High Street, Coldstream

The square church tower with its four stages, clocks and octagonal stone roofed bell tower and weathervane is a distinctive feature of the outline of Coldstream. It and the west entrance are part of the original church built in 1718. The rest of the church was rebuilt in 1905 to a design by J.M. Dick Peddie. A classical nave and aisles church with barrel vaulted roof supported by eight Tuscan columns. A fine stone pulpit sits in front of the semi-circular arch which leads into the chancel. The church contains many reminders of its close association, along with the town, with the Coldstream Guards. The King's and Regimental Colours hang in the chancel. Plaque to The Revd Adam Thomson who formed the Coldstream Free Bible Press in 1845, thus breaking the monoploy held by Oxford and Cambridge Universities and the King's printers in Scotland. Sunday Service 11.15am

OPEN JUNE–AUGUST THURSDAY 2–4.30PM

Other times by arrangement contact Dr B.J. Sproule tel 01890 882271

Church of Scotland B

109 CRAILING KIRK NT6824

Built *c* 1775 on an ancient site of worship; the bell is dated 1702. Aisle added in the early 19th-century and further alterations and additions 1892. Fine modern pipe organ by Lammermuir Pipe Organs. On A698 Jedburgh–Kelso. Services 2nd & 4th Sunday 10.30am

OPEN BY ARRANGEMENT

Contact Mrs Rose, Braeheids, Crailing tel 01835 850268

Church of Scotland B

Bowden Kirk

110 DENHOLM CHURCH NT5718

Denholm, by Hawick

Dates from 1845. Interior much altered, 1957. 150th anniversary wall hangings. Situated in a beautiful conservation village. A698 Jedburgh–Hawick. Sunday Services February–May 10am, June–September 11.30am, October–January 10am

JOINT OPENING WITH BEDRULE AND MINTO SATURDAY 27 JUNE, WEDNESDAYS 8 & 15 JULY

Teas at the Manse, Leyden's Road, Denholm on open days

Church of Scotland C

111 DRUMELZIER KIRK

Drumelzier, by Broughton

A simple rectangular building. The original date is uncertain, but it owes its present appearance largely to major alterations carried out in 1872. 17th-century bellcote on the west gable. Burial vault,1617, for Sir James Tweedie of Drumelzier. United with Stobo and linked with Broughton, Tweedsmuir, Skirling. 100 yards off B712 in Drumelzier village. Sunday Service 1st and 3rd of the month 6.30pm (except July & August)

OPEN FOR GUIDED TOURS

Contact Mr Eric Hall tel 01721 740229

Church of Scotland B

112 ECKFORD KIRK NT7026

Eckford, by Kelso

Built 1771 on an ancient site of worship, incorporating fragments of the 1668 building and the north aisle of 1724. Very sweet interior with rich turn-of-the-century furnishings in the sanctuary. Jougs, 1718, mort bell and 19th-century watch-tower. Many fine 17th-century gravestones. On A698 Jedburgh–Kelso. Services irregularly throughout the year

OPEN BY ARRANGEMENT

Contact Mrs Fish, Eckford House, Kelso tel 01835 850397

Church of Scotland B

Eckford Kirk

113 GALASHIELS OLD PARISH CHURCH & ST PAUL'S NT4936

Gala Park Road, Galashiels

Built in 1881 to plans in the Gothic Revival style by George Henderson, the main feature is the 190-ft spire. Front porch added 1922. Good glass, including some by Douglas Strachan. Stone carvings by John Rhind and wood carving by Francis Lynn. Willis organ. Sunday Services 11am & 6.30pm

OPEN BY ARRANGEMENT

Contact Dr Borthwick tel 01896 752221

Church of Scotland (via hall) WC B

114 ST PETER'S CHURCH, GALASHIELS

Abbotsford Road, Galashiels

Gothic Revival style, Hay & Henderson 1853. Reredos, Sir Robert Lorimer 1914. Stained glass, memorial brasses. Setting of church with lawns, graveyard, hall and rectory encapsulated the Tractarian ideal. ¼ mile south of town centre on Selkirk road. Sunday Services Holy Communion 8am & Sung Eucharist 10.30am

OPEN BY ARRANGEMENT

Key from the Rectory, Parsonage Road, Galashiels tel 01896 753118 or contact Mr R. Brown, 52 Croft Street, Galashiels tel 01896 754657

Scottish Episcopal WC C

115 ST CUTHBERT'S CHURCH, HAWICK NT5014

Slitrig Crescent, Hawick

A Sir George Gilbert Scott building of 1858. Reredos, J. Oldrid Scott, 1905; Chancel screen, Robert Lorimer. Some fine stained glass including two contemporary windows of 1995. Sunday Services Holy Communion 9.30am, Family Eucharist 10.30am, Friday 12 noon Holy Hour

OPEN MONDAY & TUESDAY 10AM–12 NOON, WEDNESDAY 7AM–12 NOON, THURSDAY & FRIDAY 2–4PM

Scottish Episcopal WC B

116 HOBKIRK PARISH CHURCH

Hobkirk, Bonchester Bridge, by Hawick

A Christian site for over nine hundred years. The present church was built in 1862. Stones from the earlier churches are incorporated in the font. The bell is inscribed "I was made for Hobkirk in 1745". 1 mile west of Bonchester Bridge on the A6088 Hawick to Newcastle (off A68). United with Southdean. Sunday Service 11am

OPEN DAILY ALL YEAR

Church of Scotland

117 HOWNAM PARISH CHURCH

Hownam, Morebattle, Kelso

In an idyllic situation on the haugh by the Kale Water. The original building appears to have been cruciform, but was remodelled in 1752 as a rectangle, and substantially modernised in 1844. The interior was refurbished in 1986. From the original church there remains a round-headed doorway in the south wall, dating from the turn of the 15th and 16th centuries. Linked with Linton, Morebattle and Yetholm. Sunday Service 2nd and 4th of every month 12.30pm

OPEN ALL YEAR DURING DAYLIGHT HOURS

Church of Scotland B

118 KELSO NORTH NT7234

Roxburgh Street, Kelso

Erected 1866 for the congregation of Kelso North Free Church, architect Frederick T. Pilkington. The front of the church is very ornate, being designed in the Gothic style, with the tower and spire rising to some 180 ft. Extensively renovated in 1934 and 1984–89. Although the exterior is quite massive, in contrast the interior is fairly neat and compact. Sunday Service 11.30am, Evening Worship 6.30pm 1st Sunday

OPEN JULY AND AUGUST MONDAY–FRIDAY 10AM–12 NOON, 2–4PM

Also Saturdays all year for coffee mornings

Church of Scotland WC A

119 KELSO OLD PARISH CHURCH

The Butts, Kelso

Octagonal plan church, James Nisbet, dating from 1773, and altered by William Elliot in 1823. Built to continue worship begun in Kelso Abbey in 1128. Recently extensively restored. Banners of Blues & Royals, presented to the church by the Duke of Roxburghe, 1927. Off Market Square, by Knowes car park and adjacent to Kelso Abbey. Sunday Service 10am (not July & August) and 11.30am

OPEN EASTER–SEPTEMBER

MONDAY TO FRIDAY 10AM–4PM

Church of Scotland WC A

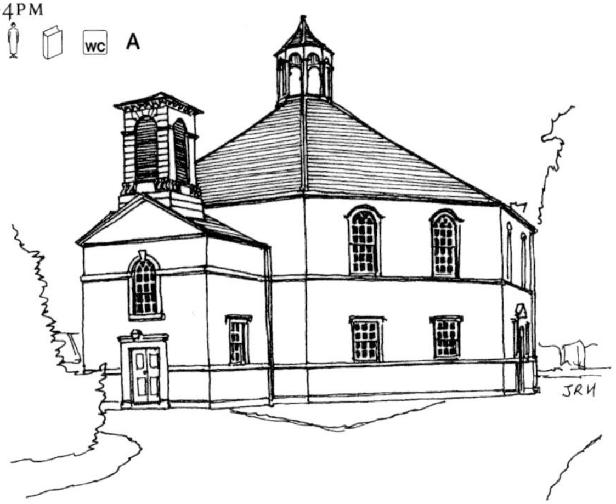

Kelso Old Parish Church

120 ST ANDREW'S CHURCH, KELSO

Belmont Place, Kelso

Situated close to the banks of the River Tweed, built 1868, Sir Robert Rowand Anderson. Altar, reredos, font and Robertson memorial sculpted in marble and Caen stone. Decorative wooden chancel roof. Stained glass. Small garden to rear. Opposite Kelso Abbey on B6089. Sunday Services 8.30am & 10.30am. Wednesday Holy Communion 10.30am

OPEN DAILY 8.30AM–5PM

Scottish Episcopal WC B

121 THE KIRK OF YETHOLM

Kirk Yetholm, Kelso

The church for the delightful twin villages and parish of Yetholm stands on a site in use since David I's apportionment of parishes. Built by Robert Brown, 1837, to replace a small dank thatched affair, it is a rectangular plan Gothic church of local whinstone with cream sandstone dressings, and a tower to the south. A remodelling in 1935, and the creation of an upper room out of the gallery in the 1970s, gives the interior a lightness belied by the sombre imposing exterior. Stained glass by Ballantine & Son, Edinburgh. The medieval bell is still in use. As the nearest burial ground to Flodden, the graveyard is believed to have interred officers fallen in that battle (1513). 17th-century gravestones. Linked with Linton, Morebattle and Hownam. Sunday Service 10am

OPEN DAILY DURING DAYLIGHT HOURS

Church of Scotland ♿ **B**

122 LEGERWOOD PARISH CHURCH NT5843

Legerwood, Berwickshire

The church dates from 1127. Repaired in 1717 and 1804. Its chancel has a fine Norman arch. Sunday Service 11.45am, 1st Sunday of each month

OPEN DAILY

Church of Scotland ♿ **B**

123 LINTON KIRK & HOSELAW CHAPEL

Near Morebattle, Kelso

On a sandy knoll, a 12th-century church much altered in 1616, 1774, 1813 and finally restored to an approximation of its Romanesque appearance in 1912 by P. MacGregor Chalmers. It retains its Norman feel and today the visitor enters under a unique stone tympanum to discover an attractive nave and substantial chancel, the arch richly carved (1912). A Norman font and chancel stalls are of particluar interest. Linton kirk is most noted for the stone above the porch said to depict a knight on horseback lancing two creatures – the stone is Norman and unique in Scotland, and legend suggests that this is the first known Somerville killing a worm. The Leishman father and son ministries completed most of the present improvements; the son Thomas also had a small chapel built in the district of Hoselaw (7 miles away) to serve the cottagers, architect P. MacGregor Chalmers. Linked with Morebattle, Hownam and Yetholm. Sunday Service 1st, 3rd & 5th of every month, and 5th Sunday at Hoselaw Chapel (except December & January) 12.15pm

OPEN DAILY DURING DAYLIGHT

Church of Scotland **B**

124 HOLY TRINITY, MELROSE NT5434

High Cross Avenue, Melrose

Built in the Early English style by Benjamin Ferrey, 1846–50. Decorated chancel and transepts by Hay & Henderson, 1900. The chancel floor is mosaic. Open timber roof carried on mask corbels. Stained glass windows in transept, 1900, by Kempe, other commemorative glass by Mayer & Co. and W. Wilson, 1963. ¼ mile from Melrose centre, on road to Darnick. Services Sunday 8.30 & 11am, Wednesday 10.30am, Evensong 1st Sunday of month 6.30pm

OPEN BY ARRANGEMENT

Contact the Rector tel 01896 822626

Occasional concerts

Scottish Episcopal ♿ 🦻 WC B

125 MINTO CHURCH NT5620

Minto, by Hawick

Designed by William Playfair, the church dates from 1830, the interior recast in 1934. Fine external war memorial. Panoramic views of Teviotdale and Minto Hill. Linked with Bedrule and Denholm. Sunday Service fortnightly alternating with Bedrule February–May 11.30am, June–September 10am, October–January 11.30am

JOINT OPENING WITH BEDRULE AND MINTO SATURDAY 27 JUNE, WEDNESDAYS 8 & 15 JULY

Teas at the Manse, Leyden's Road, Denholm on open days

Church of Scotland 🚻 🦻 C

126 MOREBATTLE PARISH CHURCH

Morebattle, Kelso

The church of 'Mereboda' is recorded as belonging to the Diocese of Glasgow from about 1116. The building was burnt down in 1544 and rebuilt; the present structure dates substantially from 1757, extensions having been made in 1899 and 1903. It is oblong in plan, with chancel, porch and vestry which seem to be additions. The bellcote at the west end is currently being rebuilt. Look for the plan in the porch which shows the archaeological work carried out in the early 1900s, and inscriptions painted on fabric on the west wall. Linked with Hownam, Yetholm and Linton. Sunday Service 11.15am

OPEN ALL YEAR DURING DAYLIGHT HOURS

Church of Scotland ♿ 🦻 B

127 NEWTOWN CHURCH NT5732

St Boswell's Road, Newton St Boswells

Church opened in 1868. Contains memorials to past ministers. On bus routes between Jedburgh to Edinburgh and Galashiels. Sunday Service 9.45am

OPEN BY ARRANGEMENT

Contact the Minister tel 01835 822106

Church of Scotland WC

128 OXNAM KIRK NT6918

By Jedburgh

On the site of a medieval church dating from before 1165. The present T-plan church was built in 1738 with bellcote, alterations and additions of 1880. A characteristic Scottish 18th-century church with plain glass and white-washed walls. Continuo pipe organ by Lammermuir Pipe Organs, 1990. Sign-posted from A68 at Jedburgh. Services 1st & 3rd Sundays, Christmas and Easter, 10.30am

OPEN BY ARRANGEMENT

Contact Mrs McNeill, Millheugh, Jedburgh tel 01835 862208 or P. Wood, Ladfield 01835 840358

Pennymuir Fair, ancient Border hill sheep fair, 1st Saturday in September

Church of Scotland B

Oxnam Kirk

129 PEEBLES OLD PARISH CHURCH NT2540

High Street, Peebles

1887, by William Young of London in Gothic style containing features from earlier church. Fine crown spire dominates the High Street. An inviting flight of steps leads up to the entrance. The chancel was reconstructed by J.D. Cairns, 1937. Entrance screen of 1965, woodwork by Messrs Scott Morton, metalwork by Charles Henshaw & Son, glass by Helen Turner. Pulpit, 1913, by P. MacGregor Chalmers. Part of pre-Reformation font in vestibule. Pipe organ by Auguste Gern, 1887, rebuilt by Henry Willis, 1937. Stained glass by Cottier of London and McCartney of Wiston. Sunday Service 10am, Holy Communion on last Sunday of month 11am, 10am January, April and October

OPEN 10AM–4PM MID-APRIL TO MID-OCTOBER

Church of Scotland B

130 ROXBURGH PARISH CHURCH NT6930

Built in 1752, repaired in 1828, with additions of 1865. Fine painted heraldic panels. Stained glass, 1947, by W. Wilson. The exterior has a pair of cubical sundials. In the graveyard the (roofless) burial-vault of the Kers of Chatto. Fine modern continuo pipe organ, Lammermuir Pipe Organs 1990. Sign-posted 2½ miles west of Kelso on A699. Services 2nd & 4th Sundays 11.30am

OPEN BY ARRANGEMENT

Contact Mrs Palmer, North Cliff Cottages, Roxburgh tel 01573 450263

Church of Scotland WC B

131 SOUTHDEAN PARISH CHURCH

Southdean, by Hawick

Built in 1876 to a design by George Grant of Glasgow on a site near to the ruins of two previous churches of 12th and 17th-centuries. 12th-century font. Super-altar set into the communion table, one of only two known in Scotland. Good stained glass. Memorial to James Thomson (1700–48), author of 'Rule Britannia' and 'The Seasons', whose father was parish minister. Prior to the Battle of Otterburn 1388, the Earl of Douglas and his army met at the 12th-century church, whence the survivors returned to bury their dead. United with Hobkirk. Special Services only

OPEN DAILY ALL YEAR

Church of Scotland WC

132 STOBO KIRK

Stobo, by Peebles

One of the oldest churches in the Borders, and of historical importance. Much of the present building dates from 12th century. It stands on the site of a 6th-century church reputedly founded by St Kentigern (St Mungo). The 12th-century building comprised nave, sanctuary and tower, the latter rebuilt from first floor level, probably 16th-century. Major restoration in 1863, John Lessels. North aisle chapel restored in 1929, James Grieve. A new stone floor laid and a meeting room formed at first floor level of the tower in 1991. Linked with Broughton, Tweedsmuir and Skirling and united with Drumelzier. Stands 100 yards from B712, off A72, 4 miles west of Peebles or off A701, 1½ miles south of Broughton. Sunday Service 11.30am

OPEN 10TH MAY AND 14TH JUNE 2–6.30PM

For guided tours at other times contact Mr Eric Hall tel 01721 740229

Church of Scotland B

133 TWEEDSMUIR KIRK

Tweedsmuir, by Broughton

The present building was erected in 1874 by John Lessels, to replace a much earlier church of 1643. Bell of 1773 still in use. Two high circular windows in the north and south transepts and some interesting stained glass. Oak for the panelling in the porch is from a tree planted at Abbotsford by Sir Walter Scott. World War I and II memorials. The churchyard dates back to the first church and contains table-stone graves of the 18th century and several other stones of interest, including a covenanter's grave and one, near the gate, to the many men who died in the construction of the Talla reservoir. Linked with Broughton, Skirling and Stobo with Drumelzier. Village 6 miles south west of Broughton on A701. Sunday Service 10am

OPEN DAILY ALL YEAR

Church of Scotland B

134 ST MUNGO'S CHURCH, WEST LINTON NT1551

Main Street, West Linton

A "Gladstone Church" built in 1851 when it served as both church and school. Unusually, the church runs from north to south instead of east to west. Fine stained glass by C.E. Kempe. Services every Sunday 11am, 2nd Sunday Choral Evensong 5.30pm

OPEN BY ARRANGEMENT

Contact the Rector tel 01968 672862

Scottish Episcopal WC

· Clackmannan ·

135 ALLOA PARISH CHURCH (ST MUNGO'S) NS8892

Bedford Place, Alloa

Delicate and picturesque Gothic Revival church by James Gillespie Graham, 1819. Usual symmetry in plan, but greater felicity than normal in lacy Perpendicular. The 207-ft spire with flying buttresses is visible from most parts of the town. Interior is by Leslie Grahame MacDougall in Lorimer-derived Gothic. Sunday Service 11.15am

OPEN TUESDAY, THURSDAY & SUNDAY 2–4PM

Close to Alloa Tower

Church of Scotland WC B

136 ST JOHN'S CHURCH, ALLOA

Broad Street, Alloa

Sir Robert Rowand Anderson designed St John's which was opened in 1869 and enlarged in 1873. Described by Thomas Bradshaw then as the 'most elegant place of worship in the County'. Early geometric Gothic with a notable broach spire. The rich interior includes glass by Kempe, and a reredos wth a mosaic of the Last Supper by the Italian Salviatti. The chancel was refurbished in 1913, its roof bearing 106 carved bosses. These. together with the woodwork of the choirstalls 1902, organ screen and war memorial are all by Lorimer. The tower contains a ring of eight bells, six hung in 1871 and a further two in 1925. Sunday Service Family Eucharist 11am

OPEN EVERY WEEKDAY 9.30AM–12.30PM

Scottish Episcopal B

137 CLACKMANNAN PARISH CHURCH NS9191

High Street, Clackmannan

There has been a church at Clackmannan since St Serf visited from Culross in the 8th century. The present church was built in 1815 by James Gillespie Graham to replace a 13th-century church. Perpendicular Gothic with buttressed tower at the west end. Stained glass by Herbert Hendrie, Gordon Webster, Sadie Pritchard and Douglas Hamilton. Modern Makin Tocatta digital computerised organ. Graveyard has stones dating from the 17th century with several Bruce family memorials. Views over Carse of Forth. Sunday Services 11am & 6.30pm (no evening service July & August)

OPEN JUNE–SEPTEMBER 10AM–12 NOON & 2–4PM

Other times tel 01259 214238

Church of Scotland WC B

138 ST JAMES THE GREAT, DOLLAR

Harviestoun Road, Dollar

A small country church with a prayerful atmosphere, set in a well kept garden. Consecrated in 1882, the building designed by Thomas Frame & Son, Alloa. The font is a memorial to Archbishop Archibald Campbell Tait of Canterbury (1868–83). Sunday Service 8.30am & 10.30am, Thursday 9.45am

OPEN DAILY ALL YEAR

Scottish Episcopal C

· Dumfries & Galloway ·

139 ST COLUMBA'S CHURCH, ANNAN NY1966
Scott's Street, Annan

Built as a Congregational Church in 1794 on the site of a Secession Meeting House and re-opened as Catholic church in 1839. Extended at both ends in 1904 by Charles Walker of Newcastle as the gift of the parish priest the Revd Lord Archibald Douglas. Stations of the Cross by Brendan Ellis, 1984. Services Saturday Vigil Mass 6pm, Sunday Mass 11am

OPEN BY ARRANGEMENT

Tel the Presbytery 01461 202776

Roman Catholic B

140 CARSPHAIRN PARISH CHURCH NS5693
Carsphairn, Castle Douglas

Built in 1815 to replace church of 1636 destroyed by fire. Central communion table. Memorials including John Semple, covenanting minister and John Loudon MacAdam, roads pioneer. Covenanter's grave. A713 Ayr to Castle Douglas. Linked with Balmaclellan, Kells and Dalry. Sunday Service 10.30am

OPEN BY ARRANGEMENT

Contact Mr Hunter Blair tel 01644 460207 or Mrs Campbell tel 01644 460208
Cairsphairn Pastoral & Horticultural Show 1st Saturday in June

Church of Scotland WC B

141 CLOSEBURN PARISH CHURCH NX8992

Built by James Barbour in 1878 alongside former (1741) church. In Gothic style with a 3-stage tower. Spacious interior with an elaborate hammerbeam roof supported on foliaged corbels. Pipe organ by Henry Willis & Sons, 1887. Window in the north transept by the St Enoch Glass Studios, 1948. Font originally from Dalgarnock. In the graveyard is the smart mausoleum built by Thomas Kirkpatrick of Closeburn in 1742. Sunday Service 10.30am

OPEN BY ARRANGEMENT

Keys from either Mrs Lorimer, Lakehead Farm Cottages or Mr Menzies, Closeburn Village

Church of Scotland WC B

142 COLVEND PARISH CHURCH
Rockcliffe, by Dalbeattie

A chaste Early Christian church by P. MacGregor Chalmers, 1911, of granite with red sandstone dressings, set on a rise overlooking the Solway Firth. Its bell tower is topped by a steep pyramid roof. A pretty interior with nave, aisle and transept and a timbered roof. Plain plastered walls are a foil for the sandstone columns which support round-headed arches springing from cushion capitals to form arcades into the aisle and transept. In the chancel, the deep colour of the stained glass window, the Ascension by Stephen Adam & Co., 1918, forms a lovely backdrop to the High Presbyterian arrangement of furnishings. Other windows by Adam & Co. and by Margaret Chilton and Marjorie Kemp, 1926. A710 from Dalbeattie, turn right onto unclassified road signposted Rockcliffe. ¼ mile on the right. Linked with Southwick and Kirkbean. Sunday Service 11.30am

OPEN DAILY 10AM–6PM

Church of Scotland WC

143 KIRKBEAN PARISH CHURCH

Harled T-plan kirk said to have been designed by William Craik, sometime Laird of Arbigland. The tower on the west wall is of two lower stages, 1776, with a Diocletian window in its second stage, and two upper stages, added in 1836 by Walter Newall, the first with a clock and the top a big octagonal belfry cupola of polished ashlar under a lantern. A Venetian window in the east gable of the tail of the church. Inside, plain furnishings of 1883. A memorial font, presented by the US Navy, in memory of John Paul Jones, a gardener's son from Arbigland, who founded the US Navy; designed and sculpted by George Henry Paulin, 1946. In the vilage, turn left at the road junction to Carsethorn. Adjacent to the school on left. Linked with Colvend and Southwick. Sunday Service 10am

OPEN BY ARRANGEMENT

Contact Mr George Fazakerley tel 01387880662

Church of Scotland **B**

Kirkbean Parish Church

144 KIRKMABRECK PARISH CHURCH, CREETOWN NX476585

Large and tall with a tower above the front gable, built in 1834 by John Henderson. 1645 panelling with Muir family coat of arms. In spring time churchyard and graveyard carpeted with crocuses. On A75 6 miles from Newton Stewart, signposted in village. Sunday Service 11.30am

OPEN BY ARRANGEMENT

Contact Mr J. Cutland, 5 Chain Road, Creetown tel 01671 820228

Church of Scotland (hearing loop symbol)

Colvend Parish Church

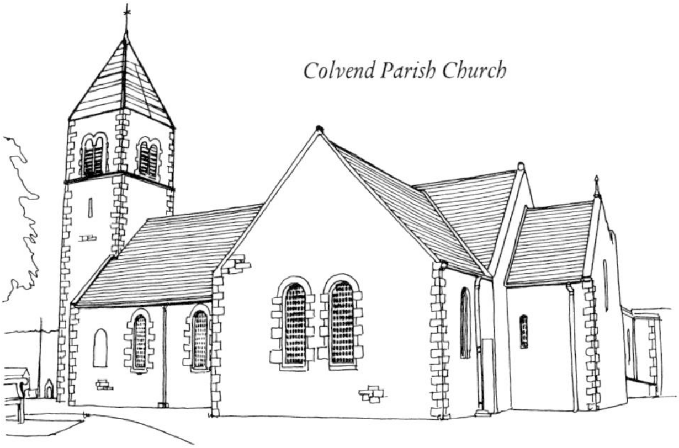

145 ST PETER'S CHURCH, DALBEATTIE NX8361

Craignair Street, Dalbeattie

Hall church, 1814, of pinky granite with red sandstone dressings. Grey granite tower was added *c* 1850. Sunday Mass 9am & 11am

OPEN DAILY 9AM–5PM

Roman Catholic ♿ **B**

146 DALTON KIRK NY1173

Close by the roofless shell of the 1704 parish church stands J.M. Dick Peddie's 1895 sturdy Romanesque church. Unusually colourful kingpost-truss roof over the nave and scissors roof in the chancel. 3–light stained glass window of the Ascension by A. Ballantine and Gardiner, 1896. The graveyard contains a late Georgian burial enclosure and the suave classical monument to the Carruthers of Whitecroft. B725, sign-posted off A75 Annan–Dumfries. Sunday Services 9.45am, 11.15am or 6.30pm by rotation with Hightae and St Mungo

OPEN BY ARRANGEMENT

Contact the Revd W.L. Kirk, Hightae Manse, Lockerbie tel 01387 811499

Church of Scotland WC **B**

147 GREYFRIARS CHURCH, DUMFRIES NX9776

Church Crescent, Dumfries

A richly ornamented Gothic edifice by John Starforth, 1868, with plenty of crisply carved detail, all in red sandstone snecked rubble. The steeple dominates both the building and the townscape. The interior is a huge, almost square space, richly decorated. Clustered shafts with leafy capitals support collar-braced and kingpost-truss roofs over the nave and transepts. Stained glass by James Ballantine & Son, Powell Bros, Camm Bros and L.C. Levetts. Pipe organ, 1921, by Ingram. Sunday Services 11am & 9.30am during summer, fortnightly Evening Services

DETAILS OF OPENING ON NOTICE BOARD

Church of Scotland WC **A**

148 ST GEORGE'S, DUMFRIES

George Street, Dumfries

Built as a Free Church in 1844 by William McGowan, and remodelled in 1893 by James Halliday who added the Italianate front of red sandstone. Almost square interior with north and south aisles marked off by superimposed Corinthian columns. Compartmented and coved main ceiling. Sunday Services September–June 11am, July & August 9.30am (Family Service)

OPEN BY ARRANGEMENT

Contact Dr Balfour tel 01387 253696

Church of Scotland ♿ WC **B**

149 DURISDEER PARISH CHURCH NS8903

Unspoilt, peaceful, Georgian country parish church, rebuilt in 1716, topped by a belfry tower. X-plan, one arm of the cross is taller and more sophisticated, built for the Duke of Queensberry and remaining from the earlier church. Inside is the most amazing monument over the Queensberry burial vault: a baroque baldacchino carved in 1695 by John van Nost to the design of James Smith who was also architect of the later church. "There are few buildings in which baroque magnificence and presbyterian decency are so happily combined" (George Hay, *Architecture of Scottish Post-Reformation Churches*). Martyr's Grave 1685. 1mile east of A702 (signed). Sunday Service 11.45am

OPEN DURING DAYLIGHT HOURS

Garden Fete June 6th. Drumlanrig Castle nearby

Church of Scotland (afternoon teas, Sundays, July, August, September) WC A

Durisdeer Parish Church

150 HIGHTAE KIRK NY0978

Built as a Relief meeting house in 1796 and remodelled for the Reformed Prebyterians in 1865, when the windows were enlarged and the gableted west bellcote and small porch were added. On the B7020, 2½ miles south of Lochmaben. Sunday Services 9.45am, 11.15am or 6.30pm by rotation with Dalton and St Mungo

OPEN BY ARRANGEMENT

Contact Mr William Cartledge, Knowehead Cottage, Hightae tel 01387 810782

Church of Scotland WC (adjoining manse)

151 ST MUNGO PARISH CHURCH, KETTLEHOLM NY1577

Built under the patronage of the Rt Hon Robert Jardine MP of Castlemilk. Late Scots Gothic by David Bryce, 1877, with a pinnacled-buttressed porch decorated with grotesque carved heads. Inside, a magnificently elaborate open roof. Organ, 1905, by Abbot & Smith. Stained glass by James Ballantine & Son, 1876. First World War memorial by F.M. Taubman. On the B723, 3 miles south of Lockerbie. Sunday Services 9.45am, 11.15am or 6.30pm by rotation with Dalton and Hightae

OPEN BY ARRANGEMENT

Contact Mr A. Leslie, Lindores, Peatford, Lockerbie tel 01576 202827

Church of Scotland WC B

152 MONIGAFF PARISH CHURCH, MINNIGAFF NX4166

Minnigaff, Newton Stewart

Church completed in 1836 to a design by William Burn. Stained glass by William Wailes of Newcastle 1868 and Ballantine, Edinburgh 1910. Font from Earl of Galloway's private chapel. Organ built in 1873, Bryceson Brothers, London. Ruins of pre-Reformation church on medieval foundations. Motte and ditch. 8th-century stone slab of Irish missionary influence. Grave stones including B-listed Heron monument. Yew tree 900 years old. Sunday Services 10am, 1st Sunday of month Holy Communion 9.25am

OPEN JUNE 13–SEPTEMBER 15 MONDAY & FRIDAY 2–4.30PM

Or by arrangement contact Mrs Shankland tel 01671 402164

Historical display June–September

Church of Scotland (June–September) WC **B**

153 KELLS PARISH CHURCH, NEW GALLOWAY NX6377

Kirk Road, New Galloway

Built in 1822. A granite T-plan church with 3-stage square tower to the centre of south wall. Interior mainly reconstructed in 1911 following original layout. Galleries on three sides with pulpit on long south wall. Linked with Carsphairn, Balmaclellan and Dalry. Sunday Service 10.30am, not 1st Sunday

OPEN MAY–SEPTEMBER, SATURDAY 10AM–12 NOON

Church of Scotland **B**

Kells Parish Church, New Galloway

154 PENNINGHAME ST JOHN'S PARISH CHURCH, NEWTON STEWART NX4065

Church Street, Newton Stewart

Church completed in 1840 to a design by William Burn. Groome's Gazetteer describes it as 'a handsome Gothic edifice'. 151-ft spire. All glass replaced 1996. Church Street is parallel to town's main street. Sunday Services 10.30am, also 6.30pm (except July & August)

OPEN TUESDAY 12.30–2PM FOR LUNCHTIME PRAYER MEETING

Or by arrangement contact Mr M.C. Dunlop tel 01671 402543

Church of Scotland WC **A**

155 DALRY PARISH CHURCH, ST JOHN'S TOWN OF DALRY NX628I

Main Street, St John's Town of Dalry

Completed in 1831 to a design by William McCandlish to replace a ruined buidling of 1771, it is probably the third church to occupy the site. Early records are scarce but a church, a dilapidated one at that, existed in 1427. Traditional T-shaped interior, plainly furnished. Pulpit with carved wooden canopy. Galleries on three sides. Stands near the Water of Ken with wide views of the Rhinns of Kells. Avenue of lime trees. Interesting old kirkyard with covenanters' stone and Gordon Aisle, burial place of the Gordons of Lochinvar. Robert Burns fashioned his poem 'Tam O'Shanter' on a local tale. On A713 Castle Douglas to Ayr. Linked with Balmaclellan and Kells and Carsphairn. Sunday Service 12 noon

OPEN BY ARRANGEMENT

Contact Mr L.A. Young tel 01644 430472

Church of Scotland WC B

156 SOUTHWICK PARISH CHURCH

Caulkerbush, by Dumfries

Standing by woodland just outside the policies of Southwick House, a stone church of local grey granite with dressings of red sandstone. By Kinnear & Peddie, 1891, a mixture of Early Christian and Norman. Its crossing tower was derived from the 14th-century tower of St Monans Parish Church. A wagon roof over the nave; the chancel arch enriched with chevron decoration. On either side of the chancel arch, a neo-Norman font by Cox & Buckley, 1898 and a neo-Jacobean pulpit. Wrought iron Arts and Crafts light fittings, once for oil lamps. Late 19th-century stained glass. Chamber organ, Solway Organs, 1958. A710 from Dumfries, turn right immediately over Southwick Bridge onto B793 Dalbeattie. Linked with Colvend and Kirkbean. Sunday Service 10am

OPEN DAILY 10AM–6PM

Church of Scotland WC

Southwick Parish Church

157 KIRKCOWAN PARISH CHURCH
Main Street, Kirkcowan
At the west end of the village, built in 1834 to replace a former church, of which only an ivy-clad east gable remains in its kirkyard (east end of village). The present church is a harled T-plan building with external stairs at the east and west gables leading to two galleries. A tower at the north side. Inside, three galleries in all, supported by marbled cast iron columns. Tall pulpit of 1834 and a late 19th-century chamber organ by J. & A. Mirrlees, brought here in 1966. Linked with Wigtown. Sunday Service 11.30am
OPEN BY ARRANGEMENT
Contact Mr J. Adair tel 01671 830214
Church of Scotland 🦽 ⑦ wc **A**

158 ST NINIAN'S PRIORY CHURCH, WHITHORN NX4440
Bruce Street, Whithorn
Built 1822 with later 19th-century tower. Simple rectangular hall church. Carved oak pulpit. Stained glass east windows gifted by the daughter of Gemmell Hutcheson RSA in memory of her father. Located on the site of Whithorn 'dig' in the former precincts of Whithorn Priory. First Scottish Christian community founded here by St Ninian, pre-dates Iona. From A75 turn south at Newton Stewart on A714 then A746. Sunday Services 10.30am and 7pm
OPEN EASTER TO END OF OCTOBER
10AM–5PM
Church of Scotland 🦽 ☐ ⑦ 📖 **A**

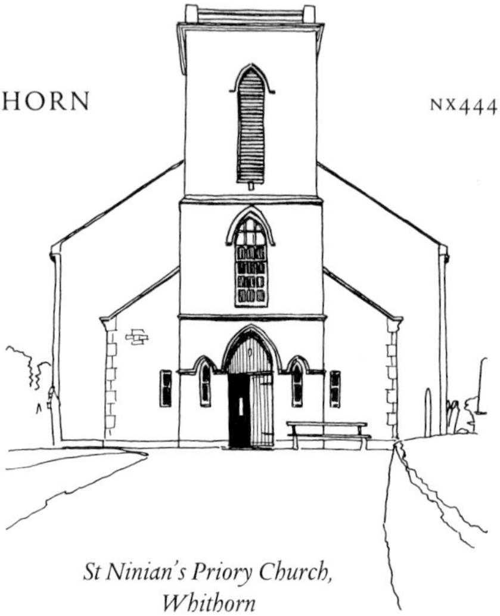

St Ninian's Priory Church, Whithorn

159 WIGTOWN PARISH CHURCH
Bank Street, Wigtown
The parish church on an ancient ecclesiastical site, largely rebuilt in 1730, was by the middle of the next century thought to be 'an old mean-looking edifice'. A new church, by the London architect Henry Roberts, was built nearby in 1851, still using the Georgian T-plan with a French pavilion roof on the tower. Built of granite, it encloses a broad nave and east transept. P. MacGregor Chalmers added a communion table and font, an organ chamber, and rearranged the seating in 1914. In the transept are three carved stones, one a Celtic cross shaft decorated on both faces with interlaced rings, similar to those of the same period at Whithorn. Stained glass in the east transept window by James Ballantine & Son, 1867. Linked with Kirkcowan. Sunday Service 10am & 6.30pm (in church hall)
OPEN EASTER–SEPTEMBER MONDAY–FRIDAY 2–4PM
Church of Scotland ⑦ 📖 ⌀ wc **B**

· East Dunbartonshire ·

160 BALDERNOCK PARISH CHURCH NS5873

Bardowie, near Milngavie

The religious history of the site goes back to the 13th century. The present church was built in 1795 on the site of an earlier church. The bell tower contains a curious panel which may have come from the nearby Roman wall. The octagonal gatehouse and stone stile feature in Moffat's play *Bunty Pulls the Strings*. The church stands at the end of a lovely 1½ mile walk from Milngavie. Sunday Service 11am

OPEN SUNDAY 2–4PM MAY TO END–SEPTEMBER

Church of Scotland ♿ (in watch house) **B**

161 CAMPSIE PARISH CHURCH, LENNOXTOWN NS6079

Main Street, Lennoxtown

Modern church with interesting wood carving and stained glass. Craft centre and old church with fascinating graveyard at Campsie Glen, 2 miles. Bus 75 Campsie Glen via Kirkintilloch. Sunday Service 11am

OPEN BY ARRANGEMENT

Contact Mrs M. Tindall tel 01360 310 911

Church of Scotland ♿ **A**

162 ST DAVID'S MEMORIAL PARK CHURCH, KIRKINTILLOCH NS6573

Alexandra Street, Kirkintilloch

The present church by P. MacGregor Chalmers 1926, adjacent to site of the original building (1843) was dedicated as a gift of Mrs Paton Thomson in memory of her parents. 2-manual pipe organ, a significant Anneessens, 1899, rebuilt and enlarged. Off A803. Sunday Services 11am & (most Sundays) 6.30pm

OPEN EVERY WEDNESDAY 11AM–2PM FOR MEDITATION AND PRAYER

Church of Scotland ♿ WC

St David's Memorial Park Parish Church, Kirkintilloch

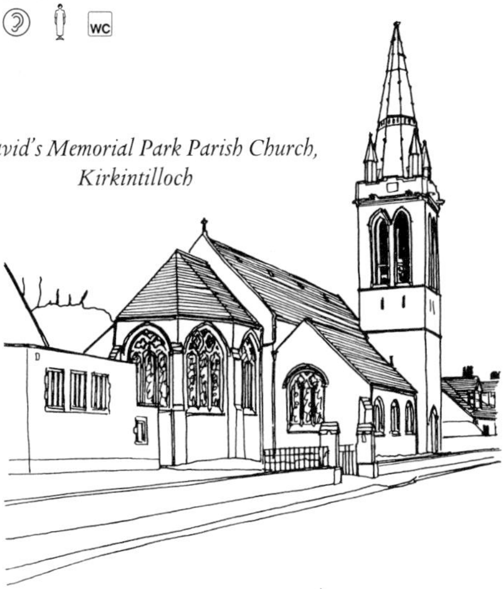

163 ST CYPRIAN'S CHURCH, LENZIE NS6572

Beech Road, Lenzie

Built in 1873 by Alexander Ross of Inverness in Gothic style with a 3-stage tower at the east end and a gabled porch at the west end. The use of contrasting materials gives a colourful interior. Painting of the Last Supper on the reredos. Memorial choir screen made in local iron foundry. ½ mile north from Lenzie Cross. Sunday Services 8.30am, 11am & 6.30pm

OPEN BY ARRANGEMENT

Contact the Rector tel 0141 776 4149

125th anniversary events 20 & 21 February, Banner exhibition, 14–16 May Flower Festival; 11–12 September Open Day and exhibition

Scottish Episcopalian ♿ 🦻 WC **B**

· West Dunbartonshire ·

164 ST MUNGO'S CHURCH, ALEXANDRIA

Main Street, Alexandria

Dedicated 1894, J.M. Crawford, architect, in pointed Gothic style. Early 20th-century addition of side aisle. Simple interior with simple altar furniture. Open timber roof with curved brace supported on stone corbels. 3–light stained glass window in memory of Agnes J. Burham of New York featuring Christ in Majesty, St Michael the Archangel, St Agnes and St Agatha. Sunday Services, Eucharist 9am, Sung Eucharist 11am, Wednesday, Eucharist 10am

OPEN BY ARRANGEMENT

Contact the Priest-in-charge, St Mungo's Rectory tel 01389 752633

Scottish Episcopalian **B**

165 ALEXANDRIA PARISH CHURCH, BALLOCH NS3979

Lomond Road, Balloch

Building originally completed and dedicated as Alexandria North Parish Church; redesignated Alexandria Parish Church in 1994 and refurbished and upgraded in 1996. Digital organ, 1994, by Allen. Off A82. 5–10 minutes walk from Balloch railway station. Sunday Service 11am plus one evening per month

OPEN SUNDAYS JULY & AUGUST 2–5PM

Church of Scotland 🦻 WC

166 NEW KILPATRICK PARISH CHURCH, BEARSDEN NS5372

Manse Road, Bearsden

Building began in 1807 on the site of an earlier church, 1649, and within the original settlement established by Paisley Abbey in 1232. Very fine collection of stained glass including windows by Steven Adam and Webster. By rail to Bearsden, by Kelvin Bus 18 to Bearsden Cross. Services Sunday 10.30am & 7pm, Wednesday 12 noon

OPEN JUNE–AUGUST WEDNESDAY 10.30AM–12 NOON & 12.30–3PM

Close to Roman Bath House east of Bearsden Cross

Church of Scotland ♿ 🦻 WC **B**

167 KILBOWIE ST ANDREW'S PARISH CHURCH, CLYDEBANK

Kilbowie Road, Clydebank

For the congregation founded as St John's on the Hill, 1897, the present church was built in 1904 on land gifted by William Black of Auchentoshen. In simple Perpendicular style, a low cruciform church of red sandstone. The battlemented belfry added, 1933. Recent refurbishment. Memorial side chapel with tapestry and stained glass window by Eilidh Keith, 1997, dedicated to the victims of the Clydebank blitz. The bell, 1933, is one of few remaining in this former industrial community of Scotland. M8 Jct 19, A82 to A8014 turn off. 5 mins walk from railway station. Sunday Service 11am except July & August

OPEN FRIDAY 13 MARCH 10AM–4PM, 7–9PM

Other times by arrangement and Doors Open Day

Contact Revd R. Grahame tel 0141 951 2455

Church of Scotland

168 RIVERSIDE PARISH CHURCH, DUMBARTON NS3975

High Street, Dumbarton

Built in 1811, to a design by John Brash, on the site of earlier 13/14th-century and 17th-century churches. The steeple and pedimented gable command the westward curve of the High Street. Urns perch on the belfry and adorn the gatepiers. The interior was refurbished in 1886. Stained glass includes the Queen Margaret window by the Abbey Studio of Glasgow and Ascension window by C.E. Stewart. 11th/12th-century Crusader stone now housed in gallery. Sunday Service 11.15am

OPEN WEEKDAYS 9.30AM–12.30PM

Church of Scotland A

169 THE CHURCH OF KILMARONOCK NS453875

By Alexandria

The present church building dates from 1813 and has a stout classical dignity. Parish long-established when documented records began; the screen at the entrance to the nave lists incumbents since 1325. Memorial wall plaques. Ancient stones in graveyard. North side of A811, 3 miles west of Drymem. Sunday Service 11am May–September

OPEN BY ARRANGEMENT

Contact the Revd Andrew Mitchell tel 01360 660295

Summer Fair first Saturday in June. Occasional events by the Friends of Kilmaronock

Church of Scotland B

The Church of Kilmaronock

· Dundee ·

170 DUNDEE PARISH CHURCH (ST MARY'S)

Nethergate, Dundee

Founded in 1190 by Earl of Huntingdon. Rebuilt 1844 by William Burn. Beautiful 19th & 20th-century stained glass windows. 1914–18 war memorial. Impressive organ installed in 1865. Reading desk with interesting history. North of Discovery Point and railway station. Sunday Service 11am, Holy Communion last Sunday of month

OPEN MAY–SEPTEMBER MONDAY, TUESDAY, THURSDAY, FRIDAY 10AM–12 NOON

Church of Scotland WC **B**

171 MEADOWSIDE ST PAUL'S CHURCH

114–116 Nethergate, Dundee

Built in 1852, replacing the Mariners' Church, to a design by Charles Wilson. It 'boasts a fine spire terminating the elevation of Nethergate before it is disrupted by the ring road'. Hammer beam roof. Organ by Walker & Co., 1902, overhauled by Rushworth & Dreaper, 1971. Stained glass, some by Jones & Willis, and by Alexander Russell. A hall complex, M.J. Rodgers, 1988. A feature of the garden is an artistic stone wall by David Wilson. Sunday Service 11am

OPEN WEDNESDAY 12 NOON–1.30PM FOR PRAYER AND MEDITATION

Church of Scotland (Cornerstone Coffee House adjoining) WC **B**

172 ST ANDREW'S CATHEDRAL

150 Nethergate, Dundee

Designed by George Mathewson in 1835, impressive arcaded interior. Outstanding 19th and 20th-century stained glass by Mayer of Munich. Sunday Mass 10.30am, 7pm. Weekday Mass 10am

OPEN MONDAY TO SATURDAY 9AM–3PM

Roman Catholic

173 ST ANDREW'S PARISH CHURCH

King Street, Dundee

Trades Kirk with interesting history, dating from 1774, Samuel Bell with plans by James Craig, Edinburgh. Beautiful stained glass. Includes Glasite Kirk, 1777, now part of church hall complex. Handsome spire with peal of fine musical bells. Lovely gardens. Teas on Saturdays. Next to Wellgate Shopping Centre. Sunday Service 11am all year, also 9.30am June, July & August

OPEN TUESDAY THURSDAY SATURDAY, 10AM–12 NOON ALL YEAR

Also Doors Open Day

Church of Scotland (Saturdays) WC **A**

St Andrew's Parish Church Hall (former Glasite Kirk), Dundee

174 ST JOHN THE BAPTIST CHURCH

116 Albert Street, Dundee

The present building was consecrated in 1886. Designed with a French style roof by the Revd Edward Sugden, 1885. The sanctuary and chancel are panelled in late Gothic style, the details suggested by the woodwork in King's College Chapel, Aberdeen. Open wood roof and pillars give this interior a Scandinavian feel. Reredos by William Hole. The font cover is a splendid carved wooden spire

OPEN THURSDAY 9–11AM

Other times by arangement. Contact Revd James Forbes tel 01382 461640

Scottish Episcopal ♿ 📖 WC **B**

175 ST MARY'S CHURCH, BROUGHTY FERRY

Queen Street, Broughty Ferry

Designed by Sir George Gilbert Scott,1858 and added to,1870. Sir Robert Lorimer extended the chancel, 1911. The pulpit, screen, choir stalls and reredos are all by Lorimer. Garden of Remembrance. On the main road from Carnoustie and Monifieth to Dundee. Frequent bus service. Sunday Services 8.30am, 11am, 6.30pm. Weekdays Matins 7am, Evensong 6pm

OPEN DAILY ALL YEAR

Scottish Episcopal ♿ 👂 **A**

176 ST PAUL'S CATHEDRAL

Castlehill, 1 High Street, Dundee

Designed by Sir George Gilbert Scott, the Cathedral stands on the site of Dundee's ancient Castle. Gothic in style, but Gothic with a difference. Tall, graceful columns give an impression of lightness and airiness. East end of High Street at junction with Commercial Street. Walking distance from rail and bus stations. Sunday Services 8am, 9.40am, 11am, 6.30pm

OPEN MONDAY TO SATURDAY 11AM–5PM

Scottish Episcopal 👂 🧍 📖 ☕ WC **A**

177 ST PETER'S FREE CHURCH

St Peter Street, Dundee

1836, by Hean Brothers. Remarkably douce for a revivalist kirk: yet this was the seat of the Revd Robert McCheyne (1813–43) a major player in the Evangelical revival, who made these sober rafters ring. An elegant, classical church with a gallery carried on cast-iron columns. Original pulpit. The plain simplicity of the building is ennobled by the tower and stone spire against its east gable. The church has served different denominations since its opening, Free, United Free, and Church of Scotland. It became a Free Church again in 1987. From city centre, west for 1 mile along High Street, Nethergate and Perth Road. Turn right into St Peter Street. Sunday Service 11am & 6.30pm. Wednesday Prayer meeting 7.30pm

OPEN BY ARRANGEMENT

Contact Revd D. Robertson tel 01382 861401

Free Church of Scotland ♿ 📖 WC **B**

178 ST SALVADOR'S CHURCH

Church Street, Dundee

Glorious painted interior with stencilled wall decoration and open roof, built in 1868 in early Arts & Crafts Gothic by G.F. Bodley. Carnegie Street end of Church Street, off Hilltown. Buses 20 & 22. Daily Services Tuesday 9.15am, Wednesday 9.30am, Thursday 12.30pm, Friday/Saturday 8am, Every day 5pm. Sunday Services 9am, 11am, 5pm

OPEN MOST MORNINGS

Also Doors Open Day September

Scottish Episcopal WC B

179 THE STEEPLE CHURCH

Nethergate, Dundee

Church building dates from 1788, Samuel Bell. Entry through 15th-century St Mary's Tower. A landmark, known as Old Steeple. City centre. Sunday Services 11am & 6.30pm (7pm July & August)

OPEN JULY–AUGUST MONDAY TO SATURDAY 10AM–3PM

Also Doors Open Day and other summer activities

Mary Slessor Exhibition July–August – details in church

Church of Scotland WC B

180 STOBSWELL PARISH CHURCH

Albert Street, Dundee

On a prominent site, by Charles Edward and Thomas S. Robertson, 1874. The buildings have recently undergone extensive refurbishment. L-shaped church. Fine stained glass windows by William Wilson. From city centre buses 15, 17, 32, 33, 35 & 36. Sunday Service 11am (10.30am July & August)

OPEN DUNDEE DOORS OPEN DAY SEPTEMBER

Church of Scotland WC B

· Edinburgh ·

181 AUGUSTINE UNITED CHURCH NT257734

41 George IV Bridge, Edinburgh

Built 1857–61 by J., J.M. & W.H. Hay with Romanesque, Renaissance and Classical elements. The projecting centre of the gable front is carried up as the 'bride's-cake' tower which is topped by a spire of three diminishing octagonal stages. Composite hammerbeam and kingpost roof. The Bradford computer organ, 1994, uses the pipes and case of the former Ingram organ (1929). Major alterations to interior, to plans by Stewart Tod and Partners, 1995. Two stained glass windows by Robert Burns, formerly in the gallery now at ground floor level. Sunday Service 11am, Holy Communion 1st and 3rd Sundays

OPEN THURSDAYS FROM 10.30AM TO 12.30PM OR LATER

Or by arrangement contact Miss Moon tel 0131 667 0071

Scottish Congregational & United Reformed Church WC B

182 BARCLAY CHURCH NT249726

Bruntsfield Place, Tollcross, Edinburgh

1864, in powerful Ruskinian Gothic, this is Frederick T. Pilkington's greatest achievement. 230-ft spire is well known landmark. Spectacular theatrical space within with double gallery. Painted ceiling. 100 metres south of King's Theatre. Sunday Services 11am & 6.30pm

OPEN JULY–AUGUST TUESDAY & THURSDAY 2–5PM

Other times and details of special events from J. Baker tel 0131 229 0899

Church of Scotland WC A

183 BLACKHALL UNITED FREE CHURCH NT2174

1 House o' Hill Road, Edinburgh

Modern church completed in 1968. A90 at the junction between Telford Road and Queensferry Road. LRT buses 32, 52, & 41A, SMT43. Sunday Services 11.30am, also 6.30pm on 3rd Sunday from September to May

United Free Church of Scotland

184 BROUGHTON ST MARY'S PARISH CHURCH NT256748

12 Bellevue Crescent, Edinburgh

A Burgh Church, built to serve Edinburgh's spreading New Town. Designed in 1824 by Thomas Brown as centrepiece of Bellevue Crescent. Neo-classical style, graceful interior with fluted Corinthian columns supporting gallery. Original pulpit. Nathaniel Bryson's stained glass 'Annunciation' is of particular note. Robert Stevenson, lighthouse builder and grandfather of Robert Louis Stevenson, elder 1828–43. 10–15 mins walk from east end of Princes Street. City buses 8, 9, 19, 39 to Bellevue Crescent. Sunday Service 10.30am

OPEN APRIL–SEPTEMBER WEDNESDAY 10AM–12 NOON AND MONDAY–SATURDAY DURING EDINBURGH FESTIVAL 17–22 AUGUST 1998 10–4PM

Church of Scotland WC A

Broughton St Mary's Parish Church

185 CANONGATE KIRK NT265738

Canongate, Royal Mile, Edinburgh

This interesting and recently restored 17th-century church was opened in 1691, its plan by James Smith being unique among 17th-century Scottish churches. Restored in 1991, Stewart Tod Partnership. The churchyard contains the remains of many famous Scots, including economist Adam Smith. 'Open Kirk' information sheets in several languages. Organ appeal. On the Royal Mile opposite Huntly House Museum. LRT bus 1 from Castle. Sunday Services Family Service 10am, Parish Worship 11.15am

OPEN MID-JUNE–MID-SEPTEMBER MONDAY TO SATURDAY 10.30AM–4.30PM

Churchyard open all year

Church of Scotland WC A

186 CARRICK KNOWE PARISH CHURCH NT203721

Saughton Road North, Edinburgh

Furnishings in Scottish Border oak, commissioned by the Church of Scotland as part of their exhibit for the Empire Exhibition in Glasgow of 1938. Baptismal bowl gifted by Her Majesty Queen Elizabeth The Queen Mother. Tapestry, Dovecot Studios, Edinburgh. Opposite Union Park. Buses 1 & 6. Sunday Service 11am

OPEN EVERY MORNING EXCEPT WEDNESDAY 9.30AM–12 NOON

Church of Scotland A

187 COLINTON PARISH CHURCH (ST CUTHBERT'S) NT216692

Dell Road, Edinburgh

Rebuilt by Sydney Mitchell, 1908, the church has a fine neo-Byzantine interior. Grey sandstone columns with angel capitals and low relief angels in the spandrels of the nave roof. The east apse is boldly screened, with an inscribed oak cross-beam. Pulpit, oak communion table and marble font all 1908. Sunday Services 9.30 & 11am

OPEN BY ARRANGEMENT

Contact the church office tel 0131 441 2232

Church of Scotland WC B

188 CORSTORPHINE OLD PARISH CHURCH NT201728

Kirk Loan, Corstorphine, Edinburgh

Interesting 15th-century church with tower, pre-Reformation relics, Scottish heraldic panels and fine medieval tombs, including those of the founders Sir Adam Forrester, Lord Provost of Edinburgh d.1405 and Sir John Forrester, Lord Chamberlain of Scotland in the reign of James I. Fine Victorian stained glass. Interesting gravestones in churchyard. Sunday Services 10am & 11.30am

OPEN WEDNESDAYS 10.30AM–12 NOON

EXCEPT DECEMBER & JANUARY

Coincides with opening of Dower House (Corstorphine Trust)

Special events during Edinburgh Festival, August

Church of Scotland (partial) A

Corstorphine Old Parish Church

189 CORSTORPHINE UNITED FREE CHURCH NT1972

Glebe Road, Corstorphine, Edinburgh

Intimate, secluded, friendly little church. Various ante-rooms and large hall. Good grassed area for barbecues. Off St John's Road opposite Harp Hotel. Sunday Service 10am

OPEN BY APPOINTMENT

Contact the Minister tel 0131 336 5854

United Free Church of Scotland WC

190 CRAMOND KIRK NT190768

Cramond Glebe Road, Edinburgh

A cruciform kirk of 1656 with 15th-century tower. Interior altered 1701, 1811, large reconstruction, 1911 by Donald McArthy and James Mather. Pitch pine hammerbeam roof, oak furnishings, white marble font. Pipe organ, Norman & Beard, 1911. Burgerhuys bell, 1619. Jock Howieson mosaic. Plan of kirkyard available; Roman settlement remains. Off Whitehouse Road. City buses 40 & 41. Sunday Services 9.30 & 11am. July & August 10am

OPEN DAILY DURING EDINBURGH FESTIVAL 2–5PM

Cramond Village exhibition at the Maltings

Church of Scotland B

191 DALMENY PARISH CHURCH (ST CUTHBERT'S) NT1477

Main Street, Dalmeny, Nr South Queensferry

The most complete example of Romanesque architecture in Scotland. Dates from *c* 1130. Superb medieval south doorway, arch stones elaborately carved with animals, figures and grotesque heads. Historic graveyard. Off A90, follow signs for Dalmeny and South Queensferry. Sunday Service 11.30am

OPEN APRIL–SEPTEMBER SUNDAY 2–4.30PM

Other times key from the post office or Manse, or 5 Main Street. Parties please tel in advance Mr W. Ross 0131 331 1479

Church of Scotland A

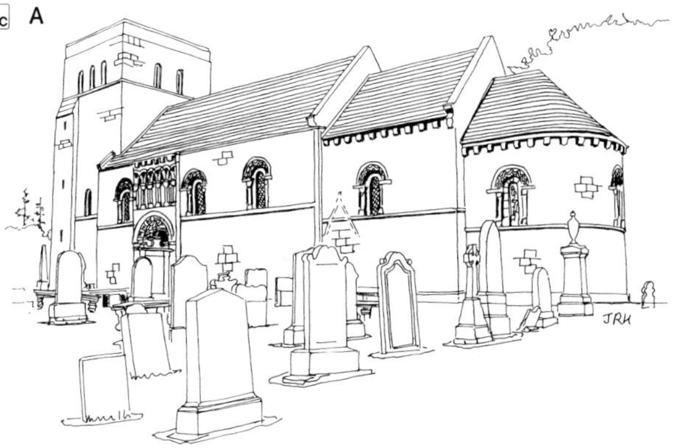

Dalmeny Parish Church (St Cuthbert's)

192 DAVIDSON'S MAINS PARISH CHURCH

1 Quality Street x Queensferry Road

Originally Cramond Free Church. A small T-plan kirk with flat Gothic windows by David Cousin, 1843. The timber bellcote with a prickly slated hat was added to the centre gables in 1866. Featureless interior enlarged to the north in 1970. To the east the little school and house by Robert R. Raeburn, 1846, were extended with a hall by Auldjo Jamieson & Arnott, 1933, maintaining the domestic scale by means of a dormered roof. Essentially a village church. Sunday Service July–August 10am & 6.30pm, September–June 11am & 6.30pm

OPEN TUESDAY–THURSDAY 10AM–2PM

At other times contact the Beadle, Mr John Brown tel 0131 336 2065

Church of Scotland

193 DUDDINGSTON KIRK NT284726

Old Church Lane, Duddingston Village, Edinburgh

12th-century church, developed in the 17th & 18th-centuries and again in 1889 by Sir R. Rowand Anderson, lying beside Duddingston Loch, south of Arthur's Seat. It has associations with the English artist Turner, and with Sir Walter Scott, both friends of the Minister, Revd John Thomson (1804–40), himself a noted landscape painter. LRT bus 44 to Duddingston Road. Sunday Services 10am & 11.30am

OPEN AUGUST–SEPTEMBER SATURDAY 10AM–4PM, SUNDAY 2–4PM

Church of Scotland WC **A**

194 EDINBURGH METHODIST MISSION NT248730

The Central Hall, West Tollcross, Edinburgh

1901 by Dunn & Findlay, Edinburgh. Several alterations have been made to suit the changing needs of the congregation. Main hall has a curved and ribbed ceiling on arches rising from Ionic columns. Leaded windows of clear 'cathedral' glass embellished in the style of Glasgow Art Nouveau. Lower landings are decorated with mosaic tiles. A well known venue for concerts, conferences and meetings. ½ mile south of Princes Street west end, via Lothian Road. LRT buses 10, 11, 15–18, 23, 24, 27, 45, 47. Sunday Services 11am & 6pm

OPEN MONDAY TO FRIDAY 9AM–10PM, SATURDAY 9AM–12.30PM

Venue for the National Association of Youth Orchestras during Edinburgh Festival, daily performances

Methodist WC **B**

195 EDINBURGH SEVENTH-DAY ADVENTIST CHURCH

3 Bristo Place, Edinburgh

A red sandstone building, by Sydney Mitchell & Wilson 1900, this church is unusual in having its sanctuary on the first floor. The rather handsome staircase is flanked by a tiled wall. The sanctuary interior is well lit by four large windows looking onto the street. Pulpit and furnishings in pine; two galleries, one of which houses a pipe organ by Gray & Davison. Services Saturday 10am (Bible Study) and 11.15am (Worship Service)

OPEN BY ARRANGEMENT

Edinburgh Fringe Festival Venue, August

Contact Pastor David West tel 0131 667 3881

Seventh-day Adventist

196 GREENSIDE PARISH CHURCH NT263745

Royal Terrace, Edinburgh

T-plan design by Gillespie Graham, 1839 with tower added in 1851, set amidst Playfair's great terraces. Connections with Robert Louis Stevenson who knew it as 'the church on the hill'. Off London Road. Sunday Services 11am & 6.30pm (no evening service July & August)

OPEN BY ARRANGEMENT

Contact the Session Clerk tel 0131 669 5324

Church of Scotland WC **B**

197 GREYFRIARS TOLBOOTH & HIGHLAND KIRK NT256734

Greyfriars Place, Edinburgh

The first post-Reformation church built in Edinburgh, 1620, altered 1722, 1858, 1938 & 1990. The National Covenant signed here in 1638. Fine 19th-century coloured glass by Ballantine, and Peter Collins organ, 1990. Historic kirkyard, former Franciscan Friary garden, has fine examples of 16th-century monuments, the Martyrs' Monument, Covenanters' Prison and memorial to Greyfriars Bobby. South end of George IV Bridge. City buses 2, 12, 23, 24, 27, 28, 29, 40, 42, 45, 47. Sunday Services 11am & 12.30pm (Gaelic), 1st Sunday of month 9.15am Holy Communion, 2nd Sunday of month 6pm Evening Service, Thursdays all year 1.10–1.30pm Lunchtime Service with organ music

OPEN APRIL–OCTOBER MONDAY TO FRIDAY 10.30AM–4.30PM, SATURDAY 10.30AM–2.30PM, NOVEMBER–MARCH THURSDAY 1.30–3.30PM

Churchyard open all year Monday to Friday 8am–6pm, Saturday and Sunday 10am–4pm. Special events: year round programme of concerts and lectures. Programme available. Tours for groups, contact Visitors Officer tel 0131 226 5429

Church of Scotland WC A

198 ST PHILIP'S, JOPPA NT313736

Abercorn Terrace, Joppa, Edinburgh

A really striking edifice in the Early Decorated style by J. Honeyman, 1877. 170-ft broach spire over a lofty belfry. Aisled nave with entry in the south gable. Inside, a remarkably complete interior. Clustered piers with leafy capitals support the nave arcade, foliated corbels on the clerestorey support the wood-lined tunnel-roof. Fine stained glass windows to aisles. Sunday Service 11am

OPEN BY ARRANGEMENT

Contact Mr Mitchell tel 0131 669 3641

Church of Scotland WC B

199 KIRK O'FIELD PARISH CHURCH NT264732

146 Pleasance, Edinburgh

Built as Charteris Memorial Church in 1912. Late Scots Gothic by James B. Dunn. Lorimerian vine enrichment on the vestibule ceiling. Wagon-roofed nave with west gallery. Memorial to The Revd A.H. Charteris 1908. Mission Hall, 1891, dedicated to St Ninian. City buses 2, 2A, 21. Sunday Service 11am

OPEN SATURDAY 5 SEPTEMBER 10AM–4PM

Church of Scotland WC

Greyfriars Tolbooth & Highland Kirk

200 KIRKLISTON PARISH CHURCH NT1274

The Square, Kirkliston

Mainly 12th-century church. Has two Norman archways, the largest of which was blocked up in the 19th century. Two beautiful modern stained glass windows. In the 19th century a small watchtower was built in the graveyard where the earliest identifiable stone is dated 1529. Sunday Service 11am

OPEN BY ARRANGEMENT

Contact Mrs Keating tel 0131 333 3298 or Mrs Brechin tel 0131 333 3252

Church of Scotland WC A

201 EBENEZER UNITED FREE CHURCH, LEITH NT266764

31 Bangor Road, Leith

The Ebenezer congregation was founded in 1891. The original church building in Great Junction Street was demolished in 1979 to make way for new housing. The present building, by Sir Frank Mears and Partners, was opened in 1984. Bangor Road runs south from Great Junction Street in Leith. Sunday Services 11am and 6.30pm

OPEN 1ST SATURDAY OF EACH MONTH 10AM–12 NOON

United Free Church of Scotland WC

202 LEITH METHODIST CHURCH NT268761

1 Junction Place, Leith

Built 1932 by Maclennan and Cunningham as 600-seater Central Hall in artificial stone and harl on site of former Secession Church. In Methodist use from 1868. Horizontally subdivided in 1987 with flexible worship area upstairs and community centre downstairs. Off Great Junction Street, behind McKenzie-Millar. Sunday Service 11am

OPEN WEEKDAYS EXCEPT WEDNESDAY 10AM–2PM, SATURDAY 10AM–12 NOON

Methodist A

203 NORTH LEITH PARISH CHURCH NT263765

Madeira Street, Leith

Georgian building designed by William Burn 1816. Renovated 1950, Ian G. Lindsay & Partners, and 1993, Stewart Tod & Partners. Impressive 2-storey 'country house' front. Light interior with galleries supported by Ionic columns. Stained glass, James Ballantine. 3-manual pipe organ, built by Wadsworth of Manchester, 1880. Small graveyard and garden. Off Ferry Road, close to Leith Library. Sunday Services 11am all year, 6.30pm (excluding July & August)

OPEN WEDNESDAY 9.15AM–11.15AM

Or by arrangement, contact the church office, tel 0131 553 7378

Church of Scotland WC A

North Leith Parish Church

204 SOUTH LEITH PARISH CHURCH NT271761

Kirkgate, Constitution Street, Leith

A church was erected in 1483 as a chapel attached to the collegiate Church of Restalrig. The present building dates from 1847, built to a design by Thomas Hamilton. Tower and porch incorporate coats of arms of four successive Scottish monarchs. Fine hammerbeam roof. Italian marble pulpit. Stained glass and emblems of the Trade Guilds. Set in ancient graveyard with interesting monuments. At the foot of Leith Walk. Sunday Services 11am also 6.30pm October–May

OPEN MAY–SEPTEMBER 1ST FRIDAY 10AM–12 NOON & 3RD SUNDAY 2–4PM

Also Sundays in August 2–4pm

Church of Scotland WC A

205 LIBERTON KIRK

Kirkgate, Liberton, Edinburgh

Sitting in a commanding position overlooking the city, a church was founded here in 1143 by David I, although there is evidence of an earlier church dating from 800AD. The present building was erected in 1815 to replace a former church destroyed by fire. Designed by James Gillespie Graham, it is a rectangular semi-Gothic building with corbelled parapet tower and thin pinnacles. A memorial stained glass window depicting Cornelius, by Ballantine, 1905. Three striking contemporary pulpit falls by D. Morrison. The kirkyard contains many stones of special interest, including a table-top tomb to a local farmer, its ends carved in relief with agricultural scenes

OPEN MONDAY–FRIDAY 9AM–5PM BY ARRANGEMENT

Contact W. Mearns tel 0131 664 4779

Church of Scotland WC A

206 LIBERTON NORTHFIELD PARISH CHURCH NT280699

280 Gilmerton Road, Edinburgh

Built 1869 as a Free Church to designs by J.W. Smith. North-east tower and broach spire added by Peddie & Kinnear, 1873. Interior with raked floor and an ornate arch-braced timber roof springing from short ashlar colonnettes with a variety of leafy capitals. Transepts entered by triple arches expressed on the exterior by triple gables. Virtually unaltered organ by E.F. Walcker, 1903. Sunday Services 11am & 6pm

OPEN BY ARRANGEMENT

Contact Mr Macleod tel 0131 467 1898. Flower Festival weekend, late September

Church of Scotland WC B

207 MAGDALEN CHAPEL

41 Cowgate, Edinburgh

The chapel was built in 1541 by Michael McQuhane and his wife Janet Rhynd. Its main features are the medieval stained glass roundels. The panelling records gifts from members of the Incorporation of Hammermen who were patrons of the chapel until 1862. The chapel is now owned by the Scottish Reformation Society and serves as its headquarters

OPEN MONDAY–FRIDAY 9.30AM–4PM

Other times by arrangement. Parties welcome. Contact Revd A.S. Horne tel 0131 220 1450

Inter-denominational A

208 NICOLSON SQUARE METHODIST CHURCH NT261732
Nicolson Square, Edinburgh

By Thomas Brown, 1815, set diagonally across the corner of the square behind a forecourt. Classical 2-storey front based on Adam's design for the west block of the University. Inside, fluted cast-iron columns support the U-plan gallery. Furnishings date from the late 19th century. Organ by Forster & Andrews of Hull. Interesting modern chapel in basement created in 1989 by Nira Ponniah. Small public garden at rear. Sunday Services 11am & 6.30pm

OPEN MONDAY–FRIDAY 9.30AM–3.30PM

Fringe performances during Edinburgh Festival and concerts at other times

Church of Scotland (cafe in basement) WC A

209 OLD ST PAUL'S NT260737
Jeffrey Street, Edinburgh

The hidden gem of the Old Town. Dating from 1884, Hay & Henderson. Entrances in Carrubber's Close and Jeffrey Street give little clue to the splendour within. Historic Episcopal church with Jacobite past has magnificent furnishings. A living church with daily worship and a prayerful atmosphere. Off Royal Mile. Sunday Services 8am, 10.30am, 5pm Holy Eucharist, 6.30pm Evensong, daily worship 12.20pm

OPEN DAILY 9AM–6PM

Scottish Episcopal WC B

210 PRIESTFIELD PARISH CHURCH NT271721
Dalkeith Road, Edinburgh

Built in 1877, Sutherland & Walker, in the Italian Lombardic style. Beautiful stained glass windows designed by three young artists in 1921. Other features of note are the handsome pulpit and organ gallery and a most unusual baptismal font. Light lunches. On Dalkeith Road, A68. City buses 2, 14, 21, 33, 2a, C3, C11, 85, 86. Sunday Service 11am

OPEN SATURDAY 23 AUGUST 10AM–4PM

Church of Scotland WC A

211 QUEENSFERRY PARISH CHURCH, SOUTH QUEENSFERRY NT1378
The Loan, South Queensferry, Edinburgh

Well used and well loved Burgh Church, built in 1894 and extended in 1993. Tastefully lit and decorated. Banners include a set from New York. Centre of village. Sunday Services 10am and 11.30am

OPEN ALL YEAR MONDAY TO FRIDAY 10–11.30AM

Access to historic graveyard (1635–early 20th century) can be arranged in advance tel 0131 331 1100

Church of Scotland A

212 PRIORY CHURCH OF ST MARY OF MT CARMEL, SOUTH QUEENSFERRY

Hopetoun Road, South Queensferry

Orginally a Carmelite Friary founded in 1330, the church fell into disrepair during the 16th century. It was restored for the use of the Episcopal church in 1890, the work being begun by John Kinross. Later work was carried out in the 1960s by Ian Lindsay. Font cover designed by Lorimer. 14th-century aumbry. Mass dial on outside south wall. Sunday Services 9.30 & 11am, Thursday 10am

OPEN BY ARRANGEMENT

Contact the church office tel 0131 331 5540.
Also open during Ferry Fair Week in August

Scottish Episcopal ♿ 📖 WC A

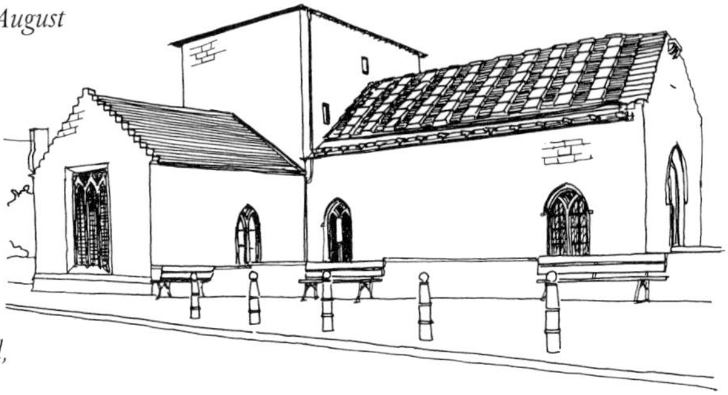

Priory Church of St Mary of Mt Carmel, South Queensferry

213 RATHO PARISH CHURCH

Baird Road, Ratho, Edinburgh

An interesting medieval cruciform church, with later aisles. The east aisle dated 1683, the south 1830. To the west of the south aisle is a 12th-century doorway, partially visible, with scalloped capitals and decorated hoodmould. 20th-century refurbishment revealed a Celtic cross stone which might suggest early worship on this site. In the south porch a 13th-century tomb slab belonging to one of the Knights Templar who owned Ratho in the Middle Ages. In the graveyard are several interesting headstones and a panelled coffin formed of a single stone. Sunday Service 11am

OPEN BY ARRANGEMENT

Contact Mrs Watson tel 0131 333 1732

Church of Scotland ♿ 🦻 📖 WC A

214 REID MEMORIAL CHURCH NT261710

West Savile Terrace, Edinburgh

Church, hall and church officer's house by Leslie G. Thomson, 1933, form an architectural oasis. A lofty, cruciform church with meticulous neo-Perpendicular detail. Stained glass windows by James Ballantine, pipe organ Rushworth & Dreaper, painting on reredos of Last Supper by William R. Lawson. Cloister court to rear with carved panel of Christ at the well of Samaria by Alexander Carrick. On local bus routes 24, 38, 38A, 40 & 41. Sunday Services 10.30am & 1st Sunday of month 6.30pm

OPEN 18, 20, 25 AND 27 AUGUST, 1 AND 3 SEPTEMBER 11AM–5PM

Or by arrangement tel Mr Philip 0131 662 1494

Church of Scotland 🦻 📖 WC A

215 SACRED HEART CHURCH NT252730

28 Lauriston Place, Edinburgh

Stone fronted building designed by Father Richard Vaughan SJ, 1860, altered by Archibald Macpherson, 1884. Holyrood Madonna of carved wood, probably late 16th century. Stations of the Cross by Peter Rauth, 1874. Buses to Tollcross. Masses Saturday Vigil 6.30pm, Sunday 7.45, 10 & 11.15am, & 8pm

OPEN EVERY MORNING

Roman Catholic WC B

216 ST ANDREW'S AND ST GEORGE'S PARISH CHURCH NT255741

George Street, Edinburgh

This beautiful eliptical church with its delicate spire and Adam style plaster ceiling has been described as the architectural gem of the New Town. Built in 1784, designed by Major Andrew Frazer. Two fine 20th-century stained glass windows, one by Douglas Strachan. Light lunches in undercroft. At the east end of George Street and one block north of Princes Street. Sunday Services 9am, 9.45am, 11am. Weekday prayers 1pm (Communion service Tuesday)

OPEN ALL YEAR MONDAY TO FRIDAY 10AM–3PM. UNDERCROFT OPEN 12–2PM

Special Edinburgh Festival programme of events. Week-long Christian Aid book sale in May

Church of Scotland WC A

217 ST ANDREW'S ORTHODOX CHAPEL NT257728

23A George Square, Edinburgh

Built in 1779 as a 1-storey and basement villa across the centre lane on the west side of George Square. Large Venetian window faces onto George Square. Orthodox furnishings and icons. Services Saturday 6pm, Sunday 9 & 10.30am, feasts 10.30am (Orthodox Easter 1998 is 19 April)

OPEN BY ARRANGEMENT

Contact Archimandrite John Maitland-Moir tel 0131 667 0372

Orthodox WC A

218 ST BARNABAS EPISCOPAL CHURCH NT290693

4 Moredun Park View, Edinburgh

Small modern church in housing scheme, 1950. Altered in 1969. St Barnabas tapestry. Moredun Scheme is between A7 and A772 on south side of city. Sunday Service 10.30am Eucharist, Tuesday 6.30pm Prayer Group

OPEN WEDNESDAY MORNINGS

Scottish Episcopal A

219 ST BENNET'S NT248717

42 Greenhill Gardens, Church Hill, Edinburgh

The chapel attached to the home of the Archbishops of St Andrews and Edinburgh. A charming Byzantine church built by R. Weir Schultz, 1907, under the will of the 3rd Marquess of Bute, to take the outstanding Italianate classical interior designed by William Frame in 1889 for the chapel at House of Falkland. Porch by Reginald Fairlie, 1934. The chapel contains memorabilia of the Archbishops since the Restoration of the Hierarchy. Buses 11, 15, 16, 17 & 23 to Church Hill. Service times as announced

OPEN WEEKDAYS 9AM–5PM

Roman Catholic WC A

220 ST COLUMBA BY THE CASTLE

Johnston Terrace, Edinburgh

By John Henderson, 1847, a single-nave building of six bays under a pitch-slated roof with a battlemented tower. Four-bay aisleless nave and one-bay chancel; the sixth bay forms the entrance and vestibule to the west end. Triple arcading at the west wall, originally supporting a gallery, now subsumed into a suite of rooms served by a new staircase. Stone altar, font and pulpit. Reredos *c* 1935 set in panelling *c* 1914. The blocked east window has been filled with a mural 'Christ Enthroned' by John Busby, 1962. Pipe organ, James Connacher & Sons, 1880, rebuilt in 1965 by N.P. Manders and 1998 by Lightonner. Church hall, originally a school, below the church. Redevelopment and refurbishment, Simpson & Brown, 1998. Sunday Service Eucharist 10am and at other times as announced

OPEN BY ARRANGEMENT

Contact the Rector tel 0131 228 6470

Scottish Episcopal B

221 ST CUTHBERT'S PARISH CHURCH NT248736

Lothian Road, Edinburgh

The present church, the seventh on the site, is over 100 years old, 1895 by Hippolyte Blanc, retaining the 1790 spire. Altered in 1990, Stewart Tod. Tradition has it that St Cuthbert had a cell church here. If so, Christian worship has taken place here for 1300 years. Furnishings include scroll-topped and Renaissance style stalls, marble communion table, murals and stained glass window by Tiffany. Display of life of St Columba in vestibule. Interesting graveyard, with many famous names, is an oasis in the centre of the city. Buses to Princes Street and Lothian Road. Sunday Services 9.30am, 11am, 6.30pm (service of healing)

OPEN MID MAY–MID SEPTEMBER MONDAY TO FRIDAY 10AM–4PM SATURDAY 10AM–12 NOON

Church of Scotland WC A

222 ST GEORGE'S WEST CHURCH NT245736

Shandwick Place, Edinburgh

Designed by David Bryce, 1869, with campanile by Sir R. Rowand Anderson 1881. Special features are the rose window and the pulpit. Woodwork excellent, mainly original. The organ by Thomas Lewis, 1897. The first organist was Alfred Hollins, famous blind organist and composer (1897–1942). City Centre West End. Sunday Services 11am & 7pm

OPEN MONDAY TO FRIDAY 10AM–4PM SATURDAY 10.30AM–12.30PM, ALL YEAR

Lunches Monday to Friday 12 noon–2pm

Church of Scotland B

223 ST JOHN THE EVANGELIST NT247736

Princes Street, Edinburgh

Designed by William Burn, 1817. Recently cleaned and restored. Notably good stained glass. Sir Walter Scott's mother, Anne Rutherford and Sir Henry Raeburn RA are buried in Dormitory Garden. Undercroft includes a cafe restaurant, Christian bookshop (multi-denominational), One World Shop, and Peace and Justice Centre. At the foot of Lothian Road and opposite the Caledonian Hotel. Sunday Services 8am Holy Communion, 9.45am Sung Eucharist, 11.15am Choral Matins, 6pm Choral Evensong, 8pm Taizé Service. Further details on telephone answering machine tel 0131 229 7565. Weekday Service 1pm, Communion Service Wednesday 11am

OPEN DAILY IN WORKING HOURS

Scottish Episcopal (Cornerstone Cafe) A

224 ST MARGARET'S CHAPEL, EDINBURGH CASTLE NT253735

Edinburgh

The oldest surviving structure in the castle built by King David I, 1124–53. Interior divided into two by a fine arch decorated with chevron ornament. Semi-circular east chancel. Copy of the Gospel Book owned by St Margaret to whom the chapel was dedicated by her son, David I. Stained glass windows depicting St Andrew, St Ninian, St Columba and St Margaret by Douglas Strachan, *c* 1930. Magnificent views from castle ramparts. Other attractions within the castle (Historic Scotland) include 'Honours of the Kingdom' exhibition, now with the Stone of Destiny

OPEN SUMMER 9.30AM–6PM, WINTER 9.30AM–5PM (LAST TICKET SOLD 45 MINS. BEFORE CLOSING)

Non-denominational A

225 ST MARGARET'S PARISH CHURCH NT284745

27 Restalrig Road South, Edinburgh

Rebuilt by William Burn, 1836, on the foundations of the previous 15th-century church. The flowing window tracery follows the original design, stained glass by William Wilson, 1966. Attached to the south-west corner is the hexagonal St Triduana's Chapel, once the lower storey of a two-tier chapel built for James III about 1477. The vault springs from a central pier, its six shafts topped by capitals with crinkly foliage. Notable 17th and 18th-century monuments in the graveyard. Sunday Service 10.30am

OPEN BY ARRANGEMENT

Tel Mr Skakle 0131 661 2510

Church of Scotland A

226 ST MARY'S EPISCOPAL CATHEDRAL NT242735

Palmerston Place, Edinburgh

Neo-Gothic grandeur in the classical New Town. Built 1874–1917, to Sir George Gilbert Scott's design. Stained glass and fine Victorian ironwork. The Resurrection Chapel forms part of the Scottish National War Memorial as is the hanging Rood (Lorimer) above the nave. 'Father' Willis organ. 300 brightly coloured needlework kneelers made by the congregation, 1990. Many other features. A8 west from Princes Street or east from Haymarket to Palmerston Place. Buses or trains to Haymarket. Sunday Services 8am, 10.30am, 3.30pm. Daily Services 7.30am, 1.05pm, 5.30pm

OPEN DAILY 7.30AM–6PM (5PM SATURDAY)

Exhibition of Phoebe Traquair murals from May by arrangement with cathedral office tel 0131 225 6293

Scottish Episcopal 🦽 ② 👤 📖 ☐ 👤 wc **A**

227 ST MARY, STAR OF THE SEA, LEITH NT272762

106 Constitution Street, Edinburgh

E.W. Pugin and Joseph A. Hansom's church, 1854 had no chancel, no north aisle and was orientated to the west. The north aisle was added in 1900 and the chancel in 1912 when the church was turned round and the present west entrance made. Inside the church has simple pointed arcades and a high braced collar roof. Access from Constitution Street or New Kirkgate. Services Monday–Friday 9am & 12.15pm, Saturday 10am & Vigil Mass 6pm, Sunday 10am & 11.30am

OPEN MONDAY–FRIDAY 11.45AM–12.45PM, SATURDAY 9.30AM–NOON

Roman Catholic 🦽 ② wc **B**

228 ST MICHAEL'S AND ALL SAINTS' CHURCH

Brougham Street, Edinburgh

St John the Evangelist

A shrine of the Anglo-Catholic movement in Scotland. The church was mostly built in 1867 but the west end not completed until 1876 and the Lady Chapel added in 1897, all to designs by R. Rowand Anderson. Austere Gothic externally but the interior is a magnificently spacious setting for a sumptuous display of furnishings, including an elaborate Spanish pulpit of *c* 1600, carved and painted altarpieces by William Burges (1867) and Hamilton More-Nisbet (1901), and a huge high altar reredos, again carved and painted, by C.E. Kempe(1889). Extensive collection of stained glass with windows by Wailes, Clayton& Bell, Kempe, and Ninian Comper. Sunday Services 8am Low Mass, 11am High Mass, 6.30pm Choral Evensong and Benediction. Tuesday 10.30am Low Mass, Wednesday 12.30pm Low Mass, Thursday 6pm Low Mass, Friday 10.30am Low Mass, Saturday 12.30pm Low Mass

OPEN ALL YEAR WEDNESDAY 12 NOON–2.30PM, FRIDAY 10AM–2PM, SATURDAYS DURING EDINBURGH FESTIVAL AND BY ARRANGEMENT

Contact the Rector tel 0131 229 6368

Scottish Episcopal 🦽 👤 wc ☕ (Saturdays during Edinburgh Festival) **A**

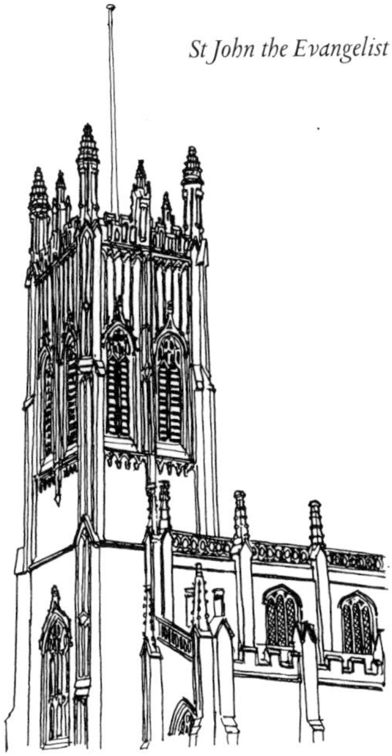

229 VIEWFORTH ST DAVID AND ST OSWALD NT244725
104 Gilmour Place, Edinburgh

Originally a Free Church. Built by Pilkington and Bell, 1871, to an orthodox four-square plan with restrained detail. The massive upward growth contrasts with the fragile shafted geometric window in the central gable. Octagonal belfry, truncated in 1976. Powerful interior, rebuilt after a fire in 1898, with very thin cast-iron columns supporting huge transverse beams over the side galleries. Organ recontructed 1976 from two instruments by Blackett & Howden, 1899 and Forster & Andrews, 1904. Sunday Service 10.30am, Healing Service 3pm on last Sunday. Shared by Associated Presbyterian congregation; Sunday Services 12 noon, Wednesday 7pm

OPEN THURSDAY 10.30–11.45AM

Or by arrangement contact Church Administrator tel 0131 229 1917

Church of Scotland (Thursdays) WC **B**

230 WARDIE PARISH CHURCH NT246768
Primrose Bank Road, Trinity

A jolly Gothic church with Francophile detail, by John McLachlan, 1892. Distinctive silhouette with central lantern and conical pinnacles. Inside, a clear-span tunnel roof. A complete and perfect set of Gothic oak furnishings by Scott Morton & Co., 1935, including the organ case (organ by Rushworth & Dreaper). Sunday Service 11am, 10.30am July & August

OPEN TUESDAY, THURSDAY & FRIDAY 9AM–12 NOON

Please tel the Church Office 0131 551 3847

Church of Scotland WC

· Falkirk ·

231 ST CATHERINE'S CHURCH, BO'NESS NT0081
Cadzow Crescent, Bo'ness

The congregation was formed in 1888 and moved to the present building in 1921. The hall was added in 1928. The sanctuary windows depict the children of the Bible. Organ by Miller of Dundee. Off Dean Road, adjacent to Douglas Park. Services Sunday 11.30am Sung Eucharist, Wednesday 10.15 Said Eucharist

OPEN BY ARRANGEMENT

Contact the Rector tel 01324 482438

Scottish Episcopal WC

232 CARRIDEN PARISH CHURCH

Carriden Brae, Cariden, Bo'ness

The first church of Carriden was consecrated in 1243 by Bishop David de Bernam, although it is believed that the parish goes back to the time of St Ninian, *c* 396AD. The present church is the third. Designed by P. MacGregor Chalmers, 1909, in simple Romanesque style with a west tower and stone spire. The bell was cast in Rotterdam, Peter Oostens, 1674. Inside a wooden sailing ship 'The Ranger' hangs from the barrel shaped pitch pine roof. Six-bay nave. Baptistry chapel with a wall painting thought to be of the Scottish School. Sounding board on north wall, 1655. A fine stone arcaded baptismal font. 2-manual pipe organ, 1943, moved from the John Knox Church, Gorbals after the blitz of 1941. Sunday Service 11.15am

OPEN TUESDAY 9AM–12 NOON

Church of Scotland ♿ 👂 WC B

233 BRIGHTONS PARISH CHURCH NS9277

Main Street, Brightons

Built in 1847. Local quarry owner Alexander Lawrie gifted the stone to build the church to a design by Brown & Carrick of Glasgow. T-plan church with small steeple with bell. Side galleries added in 1893. Chancel area modernised, 1935. Windows, 1993, by Ruth Golliwaws of New Orleans, USA. B805 4 miles south of Falkirk or B810 ½ mile from Polmont Station. Sunday Services 11am and 1st Sunday September–May 6pm

OPEN FOR PRAYER SEPTEMBER–JUNE THURSDAY 10AM–12 NOON

Church of Scotland ♿ 👂 WC

234 FALKIRK OLD AND ST MODAN'S PARISH CHURCH

Manse Place, off High Street, Falkirk

Dating from 1811, although 12th-century pillars remain in the vestibule. There has been a Christian church on this site for twelve hundred years; local legend links the earliest foundation with the Celtic St Modan in the 6th century. The square tower dates from the 16th century, and the gable marks of the earlier nave and chancel are visible. Above the tower an 18th-century bell tower with thirteen bells. Two late 19th-century stained glass windows; pipe organ of same period. 12th-century sanctuary cross. Major refurbishment in the 1960s. Sunday Service Winter 11.15am & 6.30pm, Summer 9.30 & 11.15am

OPEN MONDAY–FRIDAY 12 NOON–2PM

Lunches served

Church of Scotland ♿ 👂 🕯 ☕ WC B

235 ST MARY'S CHURCH, GRANGEMOUTH NS9281

Ronaldshay Crescent, Grangemouth

The present church was built in 1938 to replace a "tin kirk" of 1901, the architect was Maxton Craig of Edinburgh. A small hall was added in 1978. The west window, 1962, depicts the industries of Grangemouth. Altar cross, candlesticks and vases by Edward Spencer, the Artificers' Guild, his last work. Adjacent to Zetland Park in the centre of the town. Services Sunday 8.30am Said Eucharist, 10am Sung Eucharist, Tuesday 10am Said Eucharist

OPEN 1ST SATURDAY OF MONTH 12 NOON–2PM

Or by arrangement, contact the Rector tel 01324 482438

Scottish Episcopal ♿ WC

· Fife ·

236 ST COLUMBA'S CHURCH, ABERDOUR

Inverkeithing Road, Aberdour

Built in 1843 for the Earl of Moray as a private chapel for his employees in Aberdour. It was transferred to the Scottish Episcopal Church in 1918. A cruciform plan, tall and light with lancet windows. The west window blocked off by the addition of a balcony, which has recently been enclosed. A921 from Dalgety Bay, in the village on the right. Linked with St Peter's, Inverkeithing and St Serf's, Burntisland. Sunday Service 11am

OPEN BY ARRANGEMENT

Contact Mrs Clifford tel 01383 860521 or Mrs Greenwood tel 01383 860408

Scottish Episcopal WC

237 ANSTRUTHER PARISH CHURCH NO5703

Burial Brae (off Crail Rd), Anstruther

James Melville (brother of Andrew, the leading covenanter) inspired the purchase of land in 1590 for a new church, but he was exiled by James VI, and the church was not built until 1634. Described in 1837 as 'one of the most elegant country churches anywhere to be seen'. Tahitian Princess buried outside the south wall. Many interesting features. Anstruther is the birthplace of Thomas Chalmers. A917 Crail, 400 yds east of St Andrews cross road. Bus services, Fife Scottish 95 & 57, Minibus M1 & M611, Stagecoach X23. Sunday Services 11am, Healing Service 2nd Sunday of month 2pm

OPEN APRIL–SEPTEMBER TUESDAY 2–3PM, THURSDAY 11AM–12 NOON

All year coffee morning Tuesday 10–12 noon in Hew Scott Hall (converted 13th-century West Anstruther Church)

Church of Scotland B

238 BURNTISLAND PARISH CHURCH NT2385

East Leven Street, Burntisland

Built in 1592 to an unusual square plan. The first post-Reformation church built in Scotland, still in use. The General Assembly of the Church of Scotland met in Burntisland in 1601 in the presence of James VI when a new translation of the Bible was approved. Information available on the churchyard. Extensive refurbishment, 1997. Sunday Services 11am & 6.30pm

OPEN JUNE TO AUGUST 2–4PM

Other times key from tourist office or curator tel 01592 873275

Church of Scotland WC A

Burntisland Parish Church

239 ST SERF'S CHURCH, BURNTISLAND

Ferguson Place x Cromwell Road, Burntisland

Built in 1905 to a design by Truro Cathedral architect J.L. Pearson, the stone is from the local Grange quarry. The chancel is divided from the nave by a fine Gothic arch. The east end of the chancel is semi-octagonal behind a tri-form arch springing from slender columns, surmounted by a Gothic arch. Linked with St Peter's, Inverkeithing and St Columba's, Aberdour. Sunday Service 9.30am, Tuesday 11am

OPEN BY ARRANGEMENT

Contact Mrs M. McQuarrie tel 01592 873117

Scottish Episcopal WC **B**

240 CRAIL PARISH CHURCH NO6107

Marketgate, Crail

Built in 1243 with alterations 1526, 1796. Restored 1963, Judith Campbell. Pictish cross slab, 17th-century carving. Pipe organ 1936, Harrison & Harrison. Graveyard. Hourly bus service Dundee–Leven. Sunday Service 11.15am also June to early–September 3rd Sunday in month 9.30am

OPEN MID JUNE–MID SEPTEMBER MONDAY–SATURDAY 2–4PM

Church of Scotland WC **A**

241 CULROSS ABBEY NS9886

Kirk Street, Culross

Built on the site of a Celtic Christian Culdee church. Abbey founded in 1217 by Malcolm, 7th Earl of Fife; dedicated to St Mary and St Serf. Much of the original building remains, although a great deal of it is in ruins. The monks' choir forms the present parish church, in continuous use since 1633. Modernised in 1824 and restored in 1905 by Sir R. Rowand Anderson. Many features of interest. Situated in 16th-century small town of Culross. 7½ miles west of Dunfermline. Sunday Service 11.30am

OPEN DAILY SUMMER 10AM–DUSK, WINTER 10AM–4PM

Church of Scotland WC **A**

242 ST JAMES THE GREAT CHURCH, CUPAR NO3714

St Catherine Street, Cupar

Built in 1866 to a design by Sir R. Rowand Anderson. Fine choir screen, reredos and panelling, Lorimer, 1920. Town centre, A91 Stirling to St Andrews. By rail from Edinburgh and Dundee. By coach from Kirkcaldy, Dundee, St Andrews and Stirling. Services Sunday 8am and 11am, Wednesday 10am

OPEN WEEKDAYS 10AM TO 3PM

Scottish Episcopal WC **B**

243 ST JOHN'S PARISH CHURCH, CUPAR

Bonnygate, Cupar

The 150-ft spire with belfry dominates the view of Cupar from the many approaches. Built 1878, Campbell Douglas & Sellars, Glasgow when first Cupar Free Church became too small. Galleried interior. Set on a raised area in stepped gardens. Church interior redecorated in 1997. Sunday Service 11am

OPEN JULY–AUGUST TUESDAY & SUNDAY 2.30–4.30PM

Church of Scotland WC **B**

244 DALGETY PARISH CHURCH, DALGETY BAY NT1683

Regents Way, Dalgety Bay

A hall church designed by Marcus Johnston, built in 1981. Worship area and suite of halls which are used by congregation and local community groups. War memorial in grounds. Sunday Services 9.30am & 11.30am all year, also 2nd Sunday 6.30pm October–March

OPEN BY ARRANGEMENT

Contact Mr W. Wood, 13 Doune Park, Dalgety Bay tel 0138 822 529

Church of Scotland

245 DUNFERMLINE ABBEY NT0987

St Margaret Street, Dunfermline

Founded in 1072. Consists today of the nave of medieval monastic church (1150) and the modern parish church (1821) erected over foundations of original Choir. Burial place of King Robert the Bruce and numerous other Scottish royals including Malcolm III (Canmore) and his queen St Margaret of Scotland. Exquisitely carved pulpit by William Paterson, Edinburgh 1890. Fine pipe organ of 1882, rebuilt Walker in 1986. Sign-posted from outskirts of city. Sunday Services 9.30am and 11am

OPEN APRIL TO OCTOBER MONDAY–SATURDAY 9.30AM–4.30PM & SUNDAY 2–4.30PM

Abbey shop also open as above

Groups by arrangement contact Mr F. Tait tel 01383 872242

Church of Scotland **A**

Dunfermline Abbey

246 ST MARGARET'S MEMORIAL CHURCH, DUNFERMLINE

Holyrood Place, Dunfermline

A commanding building forming part of the ancient gateway to the town at the East Port. Built in 1896 to a design by Sir R. Rowand Anderson in 12th-century Transitional style. Stained glass circular window by John Blyth, stone reredos by Hew Lorimer, wood carving by Steven Foster and historical prints by Jurek Putter. Two new stained glass windows by Douglas Hogg 1998. Services Saturday 6.30pm, Sunday 9am & 11am, Weekdays 10am

OPEN BY ARRANGEMENT

Contact Father Barr tel 01383 625611

Roman Catholic **B**

247 FALKLAND PARISH CHURCH NO2507

The Square, Falkland

On the site of an earlier building, the present church was completed in 1850 to a design by David Bryce and gifted to the people of Falkland by Onesiphorus Tyndall Bruce, of the family of Bruce of Earlshall. The style is Victorian Gothic. Centre pews convert to long communion tables. Stained glass 1897. A912 Perth–Kirkcaldy. Bus service 36 from Perth. Sunday Service 10am

OPEN 16 JUNE–2 SEPTEMBER TUESDAY & WEDNESDAY 2–4PM

Falkland Festival late June. Information from Mr R. Herd tel 01337 857732

Church of Scotland **B**

248 ST LUKE THE EVANGELIST, GLENROTHES NO2700

Ninian Quadrant, Glenrothes

By J. Cassells, 1960, the church is in a Perpendicular style, set alongside a playpark in the earliest and most central part of the new town of Glenrothes. Furnished with the warmth of pine, its interior is light and airy with an unusual layout, and houses several items of interest. Sunday Services 9.15 & 10.45am

OPEN MONDAY & THURSDAY 9.30AM–2PM, TUESDAY 9.30AM–NOON, SATURDAY 10AM–1PM, SUNDAY 9AM–1PM

Scottish Episcopal **A**

249 ST PETER'S PARISH CHURCH, INVERKEITHING NT1383

Church Street, Inverkeithing

A Norman foundation, church dedicated to St Peter 1244. The present building is a nave and aisles church by Gillespie Graham 1827 attached to a 14th-century tower. Refurbished 1900, P. MacGregor Chalmers. 14th-century stone font, one of the finest in Scotland, thought to have been gifted by King Robert III for the baptism of his son the Duke of Rothesay. Sunday Service 11.15am

OPEN JULY–AUGUST MONDAY TO SATURDAY 2–4PM

Church of Scotland

St Peter's Parish Church, Inverkeithing

250 ST PETER'S EPISCOPAL CHURCH, INVERKEITHING

Hope Street, Inverkeithing

The church was built to serve the Scottish Episcopal community in Jamestown, at one time outside the Royal Burgh of Inverkeithing. The nave was built in 1903 to a design by Henry F. Kerr and the chancel added in 1910. The interior was altered in 1980 to form a worship area and hall. Set in well kept gardens on the southern approach to the town from the Forth Road Bridge. Linked with St Columba's, Aberdour and St Serf's, Burntisland. Sunday Service Holy Communion 9.15am

OPEN BY ARRANGEMENT

Contact Mrs D. Macdonald tel 01383 414194

Scottish Episcopal WC

251 KIRKCALDY OLD PARISH CHURCH NT2892

Kirk Wynd, Kirkcaldy

Consecrated in 1244 by the Bishop of St Andrews, the ancient tower offers excellent views of Kirkcaldy. The body of the church is by James Elliot, 1808. Good stained glass windows, some by Morris & Co. from Burne-Jones designs of 1886. Historic graveyard. Sunday Service 11am

OPEN DAILY DURING AUGUST MONDAY–FRIDAY 10AM–2PM, SATURDAY 10AM–4PM

Church of Scotland WC B

252 ST BRYCEDALE, KIRKCALDY

St Brycedale Avenue, Kirkcaldy

Built as a Free Church, 1877–81 by James Matthews of Aberdeen. A 60-metre tower and spire and associated pyramid-roofed twin towers lift the church out of the ordinary. In 1988, a transformed church at first-floor level was created above a multi-purpose ground-floor. Organ by Brindley & Foster, 1893. Stained glass includes windows by Adam & Small, 1881, Douglas Strachan, 1923 and Edward Burne-Jones (executed by William Morris & Co.), 1889. On junction of Kirk Wynd and St Brycedale Avenue. Services each Sunday 11am & 2nd Sunday 7pm

OPEN MONDAY–THURSDAY 9AM–10PM, FRIDAY 9AM–3PM

Coffee Bar open Monday–Thursday 10am–9pm, Friday 10am–3pm, Saturday 9am–1pm

Church of Scotland WC B

253 ST MARY, MOTHER OF GOD, LESLIE NO2501

High Street, Leslie

Originally Leslie Free Church by R. Thornton Shiells, 1879. In 1900 it was renamed the Logan United Free Church after the Minister at that time. Closed as a Free Church in 1956 and opened as Roman Catholic in 1959. 120-ft tower and spire. Stained glass by John Blyth, painting of the Crucifixion by Geoffrey Houghton-Brown. Services Saturday Vigil 6pm, Sunday 10 & 11.30am

OPEN 1ST SATURDAY OF EACH MONTH 11AM–6PM

Roman Catholic WC B

254 ST ATHERNASE CHURCH, LEUCHARS
Main Street, Leuchars

NO4521

12th-century Norman church in a historic conserva-
tion setting. The belfry was added *c* 1700, and nave
restored in 1858. Chancel and apse of outstanding
architectural interest. Sunday Service 10.45am
OPEN MARCH–OCTOBER DAILY 9.30AM–6PM
*Teas Tuesdays 10am–4pm. Tours for groups contact
Church Officer 18 Schoolhill, Leuchars tel 01334 838884*
Church of Scotland ☐ 📖 ☕ wc **A**

St Athernase Church, Leuchars

255 CHURCH OF THE HOLY NAME, OAKLEY
Station Road, Oakley

NT0289

Built by the Smith-Sligo family of Inzievar House to a design by Charles Gray. Consecrated
October 1965. Outstanding features include stained glass windows by Gabriel Loire of
Chartres. Carved Stations of the Cross also by Gabriel Loire. Vigil Mass Saturday 6.30pm,
Sunday Mass 10.15am
OPEN BY ARRANGEMENT
*Contact Parish priest at Priest's House
(Adjacent via grass path to right of church)*
Roman Catholic

256 ROSYTH METHODIST CHURCH
Queensferry Road x Woodside Avenue, Rosyth

Founded in 1916, the present building was opened in 1970. A sanctuary of A-frame design
with single storey hall and ancillary rooms adjoining by Alan Mercer, architect. Striking
30-ft high mural, painted in Byzantine style by Derek Seymour. Sunday Service 9.30am
(Scottish Episcopal) 11am (Methodist)
OPEN BY ARRANGEMENT
Contact Mr Martin Rogers tel 01383 415458
Methodist ♿ ⊘

257 ALL SAINTS, ST ANDREWS
North Castle Street, St Andrews

Complex of church. hall, rectory and club in Scottish vernacular with an Italian flavour.
Orange pantiled roofs and lots of crowsteps. Slated chancel and bell tower by John Douglas
of Chester, 1906–09, the rest is by Paul Waterhouse, 1919–24. Woodwork of rood, chapel
altarpiece and front canopy by Nathaniel Hitch, stone Madonna and Child by Hew Lorimer,
1945, marble font and wrought iron screen by Farmer & Brindley. Three windows by
Herbert Hendrie, Louis Davis and Douglas Strachan. Sunday Services 8am, 10am & 6pm
OPEN DAILY 10AM–4.30PM
Scottish Episcopal ♿ 📖 ☕ (Ladyhead book and coffee shop) wc **B**

258 HOPE PARK CHURCH, ST ANDREWS

St Mary's Place, St Andrews

Completed in 1865, Peddie & Kinnear. Unusual canopy pulpit. Stained glass. Pewter communion ware, pulpit falls. A91 St Andrews, turn right at first mini roundabout. 300 yards on left opposite bus station. Rail service to Leuchars. Sunday Services 9.30am & 11am. Evening service as advertised in local press

OPEN HOLY WEEK AND CHRISTMAS WEEK MONDAY TO FRIDAY 10AM–4PM, JULY–AUGUST WEDNESDAY 10AM–4PM

Church of Scotland WC A

259 ST ANDREW'S CHURCH, ST ANDREWS

Queen's Terrace, St Andrews

1869, by Sir R. Rowand Anderson. Fine 19th-century stained glass in the east and west walls. Two bays of excellent modern stained glass work. A Biblical Garden, developed by BBC television's Beechgrove Garden Hit Squad is part of the popular, well kept grounds for this vibrant and enthusiastic congregation. Sunday Service Holy Communion 8am & 10am, Choral Evensong 5.30pm (not Sundays after Christmas, Easter nor in July & August), Monday–Friday Morning Prayer 8.30am

Scottish Episcopal WC B

260 ST MONANS PARISH CHURCH NO520I

St Monans

Occupying a striking position close to the sea, the church was built by Sir William Dishington, 1370, with alterations by William Burn, 1828 and Ian G. Lindsay, 1961. 14th-century sedilia, piscina and aumbry. Medieval consecration crosses. Early 19th-century votive model ship of the line, heraldic bosses. External angled buttresses and 'buckle' corbels. A917 to St Monans, sign-posted. Sunday Service 10.30am

OPEN APRIL–OCTOBER DURING DAYLIGHT HOURS

Church of Scotland A

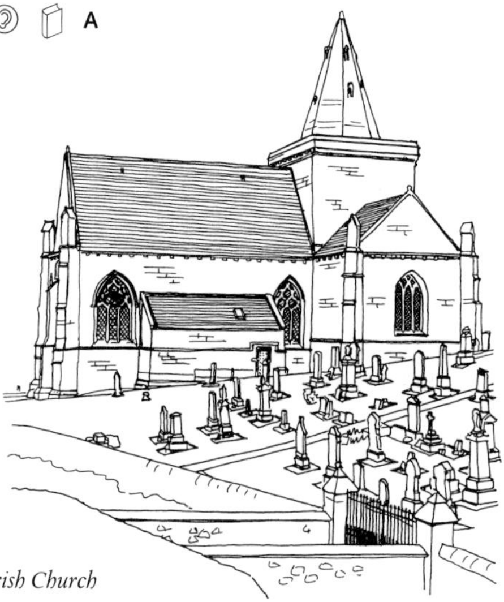

St Monans Parish Church

261 WEMYSS PARISH CHURCH NT3497

Main Road, East Wemyss

Red sandstone church, 1937, Peter Sinclair. United with West Wemyss and Lower Wemyss in 1976, now known as Wemyss Parish Church. Light oak furnishings, pipe organ, memorial stained glass. Surrounded by gardens with lovely views. A915 Kirkcaldy–Leven. Sunday Service 11.35am

OPEN BY ARRANGEMENT

Contact Mr Barker tel 01592 714874 or Miss Tod tel 01592 651495

Open in conjunction with Wemyss Environmental Centre Open Day. Guided parties to famous caves, some with Pictish and Viking markings, and Macduff Castle

Church of Scotland

262 THE CHURCH AT WEST WEMYSS NT3294

Main Street, West Wemyss

Built in 1890, Alexander Tod, simple crow-stepped cruciform church of pink sandstone. Spiral tracery in the gable's big rose window. Repurchased from the Church of Scotland in 1972 by Captain Michael Wemyss, who agreed to maintain the building externally if the church continued to be used for worship. The congregation of Wemyss Parish Church is responsible for the interior and continuing worship. Beautiful mural by William McLaren on the inner wall of the transept which now accommodates halls, vestry and kitchen. Old graveyard. Signed off A915 Kirkcaldy–Leven. Sunday Service 10am

OPEN BY ARRANGEMENT

Contact A. Tod, Corner Cottage, 40 South Row, Coaltown of Wemyss tel 01592 651498

Church of Scotland A

· Glasgow ·

Local Representative: Mrs Jane Boyd
Renfield St Stephen's Church Centre, 260 Bath Streeet, Glasgow G2 4JP

263 ADELAIDE PLACE BAPTIST CHURCH

209 Bath Street, Glasgow

Built 1877, T.L. Watson. 1995 stunning redevelopment of decaying building creating a multi-functional centre including sanctuary, guest house, cafe and nursery. M8 junction for Charing Cross to city centre, Bothwell Street and Douglas Street to Bath Street. Sunday Services 11am & 7pm

OPEN DAILY 8AM–8PM

Takes part in Glasgow Doors Open Day. Also wide variety of concerts and other events tel 0141 248 4970 for details

Baptist WC B

264 BATTLEFIELD EAST PARISH CHURCH

1220 Cathcart Road

The first church on this site was by John Honeyman, 1865 in Early-English style. It became the hall in 1912 when the adjacent red sandstone church by John Galt was opened. Spacious interior with galleries supported on cast-iron columns and a fine timber wagon roof. Stained glass includes windows by Sadie McLennan (1971) and Susan Laidlaw (1980) Pipe organ by Ingram of Edinburgh. Near Mount Florida railway station. Sunday service 11am and occasional evening service 6.30pm

OPEN TUESDAYS–FRIDAYS 9.30AM–12.30PM

Ring bell on door of glass corridor for the Beadle

Church of Scotland **B**

265 CARMUNNOCK PARISH CHURCH, 'THE KIRK IN THE BRAES'

Kirk Road, Carmunnock

Rebuilt, 1767 on pre-Reformation site, and repaired in 1840. External stone staircases to three galleries. Laird's gallery. Stained glass by Norman Macleod MacDougall. Ancient graveyard has watch-house with original instructions for grave watchers, 1828, and burial vault of Stirling-Stuart family, Lairds of Castlemilk. City bus 31. Sunday Service 11am

OPEN MARCH–OCTOBER SATURDAY 10AM–3PM

Other times by arrangement tel 0141 644 1578. Conducted tours Sunday 2pm on Glasgow Doors Open Day

Church of Scotland **B**

Carmunnock Parish Church

266 CATHEDRAL CHURCH OF ST LUKE

27 Dundonald Road, Dowanhill, Glasgow

Formerly Belhaven United Presbyterian Church by James Sellars, 1877, powerfully vertical Normandy Gothic. The congregation of St Luke's relocated here in 1960. The main front is inspired by Dunblane Cathedral. Marvellous display of stained glass, Stephen Adam, 1877, richly stencilled roof timbers, and original light fittings and furniture. Modern iconostasis featuring icons some of which were painted on Mount Athos in the traditional Byzantine style. Sunday Service 10.30am–1pm

OPEN BY ARRANGEMENT

Contact Mr N. Pitticas tel 0141 339 7368

Greek Orthodox **B**

267 CATHEDRAL CHURCH OF ST MUNGO

Castle Street, Glasgow

Dedicated in 1136, the largest and most complete of Scotland's medieval cathedrals still in use. Medieval stone screen. Crypt with shrine of St Mungo. Modern tapestry. Sunday Services 11am & 6.30pm

OPEN DAILY APRIL–SEPTEMBER 9.30AM–1PM 2–6PM, SUNDAY 2–5PM, OCTOBER–MARCH 9.30AM–1PM 2–4PM, SUNDAY 2–4PM

Light lunches etc in adjacent St Mungo's Museum

Church of Scotland A

268 CROFTFOOT PARISH CHURCH

318 Croftpark Avenue, Glasgow

Keppie & Henderson, 1936. A neat Byzantine design in red brick with ashlar facings. Carved patterns, symbolising scriptural themes, decorate the main door portico, nave and chancel columns and chancel furnishings. The bell is the Second World War memorial. 10 minute walk from Croftfoot railway station. Sunday Services 11am & 6.30pm

OPEN MONDAY–FRIDAY 9AM–NOON & 1.30–4PM EXCEPT PUBLIC HOLIDAYS

Tours contact Mr W. Yule 0141 637 7613

Church of Scotland

(Wednesday am) B

Croftfoot Parish Church

269 GARNETHILL SYNAGOGUE

129 Hill Street, Glasgow

Opened in 1879, the first purpose-built synagogue in Scotland. It was designed by John McLeod of Glasgow in Romanesque-cum-Byzantine style. A round-arched portal with highly decorated orders leads to the body of the synagogue. Ladies' gallery is carried on octagonal piers with ornate Byzantine capitals. Stained glass by J.B. Bennet & Sons. Refurbished in 1996. From Sauchiehall Street walk up Garnet Street to Hill Street. Services Saturday 10am, Jewish Festivals 9.30am

OPEN BY ARRANGEMENT

Contact the caretaker, Mr Gibson, 32 Minerva Street, Glasgow G3 8LD *tel 0141 204 1236*

Scottish Jewish Archives open by arrangement tel 0141 332 4911

Jewish (three steps) B

270 GLASGOW INTERNATIONAL AIRPORT CHAPEL

Second Floor, Terminal Building, Glasgow Airport

A recent addition to Glasgow Airport, open to passengers and staff of all faiths and creeds. Christian Services are announced 30 minutes in advance by public address

OPEN AT ALL TIMES

Non-denominational

271 GOVAN OLD PARISH CHURCH (ST CONSTANTINE'S)

866 Govan Road, Glasgow

Affectionately called 'the people's cathedral'. Set well back in a churchyard of great antiquity, the present building of 1888 is by Robert Rowand Anderson, the last in a long series of churches on this site. Its style is Early English in the Scottish manner, with details based on Pluscarden Priory near Elgin. A set of twelve windows by Charles E. Kempe. Good stained glass also in the Steven Chapel and baptistry. In the west transept is a large collection of Early medieval sculpture including hogback stones, cross-shafts, cross slabs and the richly ornamented Govan Sarcophagus. City buses and underground to Govan Station. Sunday Service 11am, also 6.30pm last Sunday. Monday to Friday 10am

OPEN WITH GUIDED TOURS BY ARRANGEMENT

Contact the Church Secretary tel 0141 445 1941

Church of Scotland WC **A**

Govan Old Parish Church (St Constantine's)

272 HIGH CARNTYNE PARISH CHURCH

358 Carntynehall Road, Glasgow

First church extension charge of Church of Scotland. Congregation met in 'the hut' until building was completed, by J. Taylor Thomson, 1932. Original single bell still in use. Extensive suite of halls built alongside the church in 1955. Buses 41, 42, 51, 20A. Services Sunday 11am & 6.30pm, Wednesday 9.30am

OPEN DAILY 10AM–12 NOON

Church of Scotland (by arrangement) WC **B**

273 HILLHEAD BAPTIST CHURCH

Cresswell Street, off Byres Road, Glasgow

Designed by T.L. Watson, 1883, in Greek Revival style. The impressive harmony and richness of the original dark woodwork and pews gives an intimacy to this interior where sunlight is filtered through delicately coloured glass. Fine Lewis pipe organ. Near to Botanic Gardens. Sunday Service 11am & 6.30pm

OPEN TUESDAY–FRIDAY 12 NOON–2PM

Baptist **B**

274 HYNDLAND PARISH CHURCH

79 Hyndland Road, Glasgow

William Leiper, 1887 in red Ballochmyle sandstone. Timber roof and columns with richly carved foliage capitals. Gleaming original terrazzo floor. Original furnishings, Henry Willis pipe organ, and fine stained glass, including windows by Douglas Strachan, Gordon Webster, William Wilson and Sax Shaw. Major refurbishment, 1997 including lighting of timber roof. City buses 44, 59, also by rail and underground. Sunday Service 11am (10.30am July & August) also October to Easter 7pm

OPEN EASILY BY ARRANGEMENT

Contact Church Officer next door, Mr Harry MacDonald tel 0141 338 6705

Church of Scotland ♿ ② 📖 ☐ 🍴 wc **A**

275 JORDANHILL PARISH CHURCH

28 Woodend Drive, Glasgow

Church, 1905 and hall, west aisle and gallery, 1923 by James Miller in Perpendicular style. Battlemented and pinnacled tower. Mock hammerbeam roof spans the broad interior. Further extensions to hall, 1971 and sanctuary refurbishment, 1980 by Wylie Shanks. Organ by Lewis, 1923. Woodend Drive is off Crow Road (A739 Clyde Tunnel to Bearsden). Sunday Services 9.30 & 11am and 1st Sunday 6.30pm

OPEN TUESDAY–FRIDAY 8.30AM–NOON OR TEL 0141 959 2496

Church of Scotland ♿ ② 🍴 📖 wc **B**

276 ST JOHN'S RENFIELD, KELVINDALE

Beaconsfield Road, Kelvindale, Glasgow

Bold and striking church in a commanding position. Topped by an openwork flèche, the stonework has the understated detail characteristic of its time, 1931 (architect James Taylor Thomson). Light and lofty interior, complete with original fitments, and stained glass by Douglas Strachan and Gordon Webster. Turn off Great Western Road to Kelvindale. Sunday Services 11am all year, 8.30pm September–Easter and first Sunday of month Easter–August

OPEN 9.30AM–12.30PM WEDNESDAY THURSDAY FRIDAY

Church of Scotland ♿ ② wc **B**

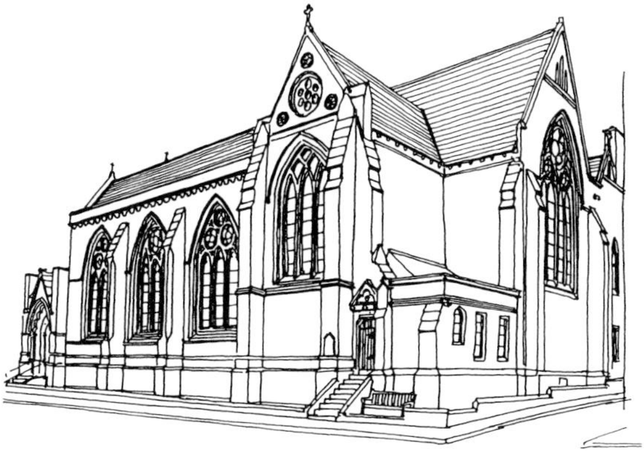

Hyndland Parish Church

277 KELVINSIDE HILLHEAD PARISH CHURCH

Observatory Road, Dowanhill, Glasgow

1876 by James Sellars, the design is said to have been much influenced by William Leiper. A tall apsed church, the west front is full of carving. The interior was recast in 1921 by P. MacGregor Chalmers. Communion table of Rochette marble. Good stained glass by Burne-Jones for William Morris & Co., 1893 and Sadie McLennan, 1958. Organ by H. Willis & Son, 1876, restored in 1930. At junction of Saltoun Street with Observatory Road. City buses and underground to Hillhead. Sunday Services 11am, also October to May 6.30pm

OPEN SATURDAY 10.30AM–12.30PM ALL YEAR

Other times contact the Minister tel 0141 339 2865.
Venue for many concerts

Church of Scotland A

Kelvinside Hillhead Parish Church

278 KING'S PARK PARISH CHURCH

242 Castlemilk Road, Glasgow

Red brick with stone dressings, Romanesque in style by Hutton & Taylor, 1932, an innovation in church design specially evolved by the Presbytery of Glasgow. The commission was the result of an architectural competition. Notable collection of stained glass windows by Sadie McLennan, Gordon Webster, Douglas Hamilton and others. Set in a pleasant small garden. Ample parking. By rail to King's Park or Croftfoot, 10 mins walk. City buses 12, 22 to Castlemilk Road. Sunday Services 11am & 6.30pm, 10.30am only July–August

OPEN MONDAY TO FRIDAY 9.30AM–12 NOON, ALL YEAR EXCEPT PUBLIC HOLIDAYS

Tours contact Mr R. Pitman tel 0141 649 4301

Church of Scotland (Tues am) A

279 LANSDOWNE PARISH CHURCH

416 Great Western Road, Glasgow

Built 1863 to a design by John Honeyman. Spire 218-ft, one of the slimmest in Europe, a powerful landmark on Great Western Road. Pulpit said to be highest free-standing in Scotland. Box pews. Beautiful stained glass, Alfred and Gordon Webster, and war memorial frieze by Evelyn Beale. Pipe organ 1911, Norman & Beard, said to have the finest tuba rank in Glasgow with some wonderful flutes. On corner with Park Road, opposite Kelvinbridge underground. City buses 20, 66, 51, 11 from city centre. Sunday Service 11am (creche available)

OPEN BY ARRANGEMENT

Also Glasgow Doors Open Day.
Contact the Minister tel 0141 339 2794 or Mr J. Stuart tel 0141 339 2678

Church of Scotland WC A

280 ST JAMES'S PARISH CHURCH, POLLOK

183 Meiklerig Crescent, Pollok, Glasgow

Church built 1895 as Pollokshields Titwood Church, and moved stone by stone from its original site 4 miles away by Thomson, McCrae & Sanders, and rededicated in 1953. Congregation worshipped in a school hall and then in a wooden hut until the building was completed. Good stained glass. 91 bus from Glasgow city centre. M8, Junction for Paisley Road West. Sunday Service 11am

OPEN SATURDAYS 10AM–12 NOON

Close to Pollok House, the Burrell Collection, Crookston Castle and Ross Hall

Church of Scotland WC **B**

281 QUEEN'S PARK BAPTIST CHURCH

180 Queen's Drive and Balvicar Drive, Glasgow

'QP', an evangelical-charismatic church, is a changing church and recent years have seen significant growth which parallels spiritual renewal in the fellowship, preaching, ministry, outreach and worship. Since October 1995, the church occupies two near-by sites: a Romanesque building(Camphill), McKissack & Rowan, 1887 and a French Gothic building (Queen's Drive), William Leiper, 1876. The interiors of both buildings have been significantly modernised and renovated to make them relevant places for Christian worship and work in the 21st century. Queen's Drive/Pollokshaws Road, 2 mins. from Queen's Park Station. Sunday Services 10.30am, & 6.30pm

OPEN SUNDAYS AND OTHER TIMES BY ARRANGEMENT

Contact Dr J. Brooks tel 0141 423 3962

Baptist WC **A** (Camphill) **B** (Queen's Drive)

282 RENFIELD ST STEPHEN'S PARISH CHURCH AND CENTRE

260 Bath Street, Glasgow

Designed as an Independent Chapel by London architect J.T. Emmett in 1852 in Decorated Gothic style. Built in beautiful polished Kenmuir sandstone with a tall clerestoreyed nave supported on clustered columns with finely moulded capitals and arches, each with carved musical angels. The main stained glass windows are by Norman Macdougall, 1905, and represent the Apostles flanking Christ in Glory. The Gothic furnishings are post First World War. Side chapel and extensive halls were added by Munro & Partners in the 1960s. Small garden with fountain. Sunday Services 11am & 7pm

OPEN DAILY 8AM–7PM

Oasis Restaurant open 8am–7pm

Church of Scotland WC

283 ST ALOYSIUS CHURCH

23 Rose Street, Glasgow

Fine late-Renaissance style church, designed in 1910 by Belgian-born architect Charles Menart, with a 150-ft campanile, domed crossing and ornate marble-lined interior. The church is in the care of the Jesuit Order, and Jesuit saints figure in the stained glass. The shrine of St John Ogilvie SJ is in the east transept, with mosaics depicting his martyrdom in Glasgow in 1615. Near Glasgow School of Art and Sauchiehall Street. Final phase of a major restoration programme in progress. Sunday Services 9am, 10.30am, 12 noon (sung) & 9pm

OPEN 7.30AM–6.30PM MONDAY–SATURDAY

Recitals by major choirs as advertised

Roman Catholic WC A

284 ST ALPHONSUS CHURCH

217 London Road, Glasgow

A late work by Peter Paul Pugin, 1905. Rock-faced sandstone screen facade. The tracery in the gable window formalised into a saltire cross. Inside, the nave arcades have polished granite piers. 150th anniversary commemorative window, 1996, by Lorraine Lamond. Church is in the middle of the "Barras", 500m east of Glasgow Cross. Services Saturday 5pm (Vigil), Sundays 10am, 11am, 12 noon, 5.30pm

OPEN MONDAY–FRIDAY 12 NOON–2PM, SATURDAY & SUNDAY 9AM–6PM

Roman Catholic WC B

285 ST BRIDE'S CHURCH

69 Hyndland Road, Glasgow

Designed by G.F. Bodley, who built the chancel (1904), the nave (1907) and part of the north aisle. H.O. Tarbolton completed the church (1913–16) including rebuilding part of the nave, and adding two north aisles and the tower. The interior scheme is mainly Bodley's. Carved woodwork by Scott Morton & Co. Sculpture of Our Lady and Child by Eric Gill, 1915. 2-manual organ by Hill. Sunday Services Sung Eucharist 10.30am, daily Eucharist times vary

OPEN BY ARRANGEMENT

Contact Mr Rae tel 0141 333 0857

Occasional Choral Evensong, usually with visiting choirs and concerts as advertised

Scottish Episcopal WC B

286 ST COLUMBA'S CHURCH

74 Hopehill Road, Glasgow

By Gillespie, Kidd & Coia, completed in 1941, the year of the Clydebank and Govan blitz, and the cost met by the families of the area, each of whom paid 6d per brick. Italian Romanesque style with an imposing west front. Sculpture of the Paschal Lamb over central door. Painted panels of the Stations of the Cross by Hugh Adam Crawford, from the Catholic Pavilion at the Glasgow Empire Exhibition, 1938. In the sanctuary a marble reredos with a carved crucifix by Benno Schotz. North of St George's Cross, via Maryhill Road. Saturday Vigil Mass 6pm, Sunday Mass 11am (children's Mass)

OPEN AT ANY TIME BY CONTACTING THE PRIEST IN THE HOUSE ADJACENT

Roman Catholic A

287 ST MARY'S CATHEDRAL

300 Great Western Road, Glasgow

Fine Gothic revival church by Sir George Gilbert Scott with outstanding contemporary murals by Gwyneth Leech and newly restored Phoebe Traquair reredos. 3-manual pipe organ. Glasgow's only full peal of bells. A82, ¼ mile west of St George's Cross. 2 mins walk Kelvinbridge Underground. Sunday Services 8am Eucharist, 10am Sung Eucharist, 12 noon Eucharist, 6.30pm Choral Evensong

OPEN DAILY 9.30AM–5.30PM

Scottish Episcopal WC A

288 ST MUNGO'S CHURCH

Parson Street, Glasgow

Designed by the London architect George Goldie, 1869, in early-Gothic style. The church is in the care of the Passionist congregation. Five apsidal chapels include St Paul of the Cross – founder of the Passionists – St Margaret of Scotland, and Our Lady of Sorrows which has a Portuguese polychrome wood statue. Late 19th-century stained glass. Gothic style timber confessionals. Opposite Charles Rennie Mackintosh's Martyrs School, and five minutes walk from Glasgow Cathedral and the St Mungo Museum. Sunday Service 10am,12 noon & 7pm

OPEN MONDAY–FRIDAY 9.30AM–1PM 5.30–6.30PM, SATURDAY 9.30AM–1PM 4.30–8PM, SUNDAY 9.30AM–1PM 6.30–8PM

Roman Catholic WC B

289 ST NINIAN'S CHURCH, POLLOKSHIELDS

1 Albert Drive, Pollokshields, Glasgow

The foundation stone of St Ninian's was laid on September 16th 1872, and building commenced to a design by David Thomson. Completed in 1877, and extended west in 1887. The apse is decorated with frescoes painted by William Hole, 1901, and the charming little sacristy designed by H.D. Wilson, a member of the congregation, in 1914. Good stained glass including windows by Heaton, Butler & Bayne. The windows in the chancel represent The Gospel Story, by Stephen Adam. Sunday Service Holy Communion (said) 8.30am, Sung Eucharist and Sermon 10.15am, Evening Prayer (said) 6.30pm

OPEN BY ARRANGEMENT

Contact Mrs Y. Grieve tel 0141 638 7254

Scottish Episcopal B

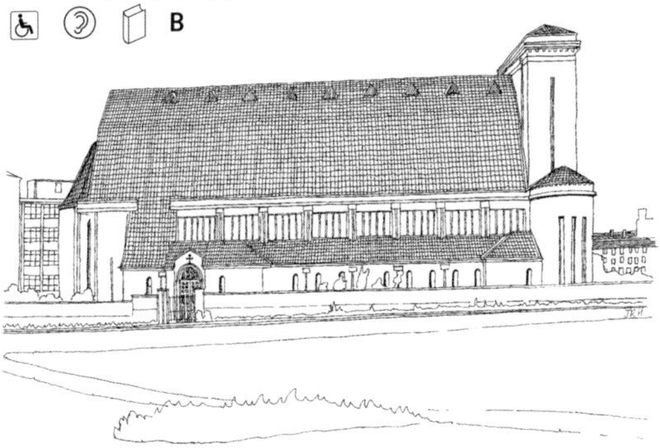

St Columba's Church, Glasgow

290 ST VINCENT STREET–MILTON FREE CHURCH

265 St Vincent Street, Glasgow

Alexander Thomson's masterpiece, distinctive Victorian Presbyterian church, designed in the classical style, and embellished by a unique Thomsonian combination of Egyptian, Indian and Assyrian influences, 1859. Owned by Glasgow City Council. Sunday Services 11am & 6.30pm

OPEN BY APPOINTMENT

Also Doors Open Day. Contact Mr Sieczowskitel 0141 649 1563

Free Church of Scotland WC A

291 SHAWLANDS UNITED REFORMED CHURCH, GLASGOW

111 Moss-side Road, Shawlands, Glasgow

Formerly a Churches of Christ church, by Miller & Black 1908, in red sandstone. Open baptistry. 300 yards from Shawlands Cross. Sunday Service 11am

OPEN THURSDAY 10.30–11.30AM

United Reformed

292 SHERBROOKE ST GILBERT'S CHURCH, POLLOKSHIELDS

240 Nithsdale Road, Pollokshields, Glasgow

The original building by William Forsyth McGibbon was ravaged by fire in 1994, its centenary year. Now the church is restored, by James Cuthbertson, architect. The interior features the work of Scottish craftsmen: stained glass windows, inspired by the themes of creation, the Cross and rebirth, by Stained Glass Design Partnership, Kilmaurs; 3-manual pipe organ by Lammermuir Pipe Organs; pulpit, tables and font by Bill Nimmo, East Lothian. Close to Dumbreck railway station, and on 59 bus route. Sunday Service 11am

OPEN BY ARRANGEMENT

Contact the Church Officer tel 0141 427 1968

Church of Scotland B

293 SHETTLESTON METHODIST CHURCH

1104 Shettleston Road, Glasgow

Former Primitive Methodist Church of 1902 which replaced a tin tabernacle of 1889. The Church incorporates windows from the former Parkhead Methodist Church. Opposite Shettleston Police Station. Services Sunday 11am,Tuesday 10.30am

OPEN BY ARRANGEMENT

Contact the church office 0141 778 5063

Methodist WC

294 SHETTLESTON OLD PARISH CHURCH

111 Killin Street, Shettleston, Glasgow

Church by W.F. McGibbon, opened in 1903 as Free Church. Fine collection of stained glass, including windows by Alfred Webster and Gordon Webster. Fine 2-manual organ. Train to Shettleston. City buses 8, 61, 61A, 61B. Sunday Service 11am

OPEN BY ARRANGEMENT

Contact the Church Officer tel 0141 778 2484

Church of Scotland WC B

295 UNIVERSITY MEMORIAL CHAPEL

The Square, Glasgow University, Glasgow

1923–27 by Sir J.J. Burnet in Scots Gothic and in harmony with the University buildings of Sir George Gilbert Scott. The structure is reinforced concrete, faced with stone. Tall interior with sculpture by Archibald Dawson. Ten of the stained glass windows are by Douglas Strachan in a cycle depicting the whole of human life as a spiritual enterprise. Other windows by Gordon Webster and Lawrence Lee. The chapel incorporates the Lion and Unicorn Stair salvaged from the Old College. Sunday Service 11am, Monday–Friday 8.45am

OPEN 9AM–5PM MONDAY–FRIDAY, 9AM–NOON SATURDAY

Chapel Choir Service December. Tours available from visitors' centre

Ecumenical (all in visitors' centre) **A**

296 WELLINGTON CHURCH

University Avenue, Glasgow

T.L. Watson's Roman Classical church with mighty Corinthian columned portico, 1884. Renaissance style interior with fine plaster ceilings. Pipe organ Forster & Andrews. Refectory situated in crypt. City buses 44, 59. Underground to Hillhead or Kelvingrove, 10mins walk. Sunday Services 11am & 7pm

OPEN MAY–SEPTEMBER MONDAY–SATURDAY 12 NOON–2PM

Crypt open Monday to Friday during University term. Also Glasgow Doors Open Day

Church of Scotland (& lunch during term time) WC **A**

Wellington Church

297 WOODLANDS METHODIST CHURCH

229 Woodlands Road, Glasgow

Built for Swedenborgians by David Barclay, 1909, in use by Methodists since 1977. A wide stair with good Art Noveau tiles leads to the church. 1876 organ from Cathedral Street Swedenborgian Church, amalgamated with pipes from Willis organ at St John's, Sauchiehall Street. Windows by Guthrie & Wells and George Benson, and war memorial window from St John's. Nearest rail station Charing Cross. Services Sunday 11am, Tuesday 12.30pm

OPEN BY ARRANGEMENT

Contact the church office 0141 332 7779

Methodist WC

· Highlands & Islands ·

298 ST MARY'S CHURCH, BEAULY

High Street, Beauly

Nave, chancel and north aisle, and adjoining house, built as a unit in red sandstone. 1864, probably by Joseph A. Hansom. Nearby the ruins of Beauly Priory, founded for Valliscaulian monks in 1230. Also serves St Mary's, Eskadale and Our Lady and St Bean, Marydale. Sunday Mass 11am

OPEN EASTER–SEPTEMBER

Other times call at Priest's house adjoining

Roman Catholic **B**

299 CROICK CHURCH

NH457915

Ardgay, Strathcarron

Harled T-plan 'Parliamentary' Church built by James Smith, 1827, one of the few Parliamentary churches still in use in its original form. Furnishings virtually unchanged since first built; old-style long communion table. East window has messages scratched in 1845 by evicted inhabitants of Glencalvie. Ardgay is 10 miles west of A9/A836 (signed). Sunday Services 2nd Sunday May–September 3pm, Communion 2nd Sunday in July 3pm

OPEN DURING DAYLIGHT HOURS

Pictish broch in church glebe

Church of Scotland **A**

300 DORNOCH CATHEDRAL

NH797897

Dornoch

Cathedral founded by Bishop Gilbert de Moravia in 13th Century, the first service in the building was held in 1239. The medieval masonry of the chancel and the crossing piers remains mostly intact today. The nave was destroyed by fire in 1570, the transepts and choir were reroofed, 1616 and the nave rebuilt, 1837. In 1924 the interior stonework was exposed. Lavish display of stained glass, including several windows by James Ballantine, others by Percy Bacon and the St Gilbert window by Crear McCartney 1989. Sunday Services 11am all year, 8.30pm summer months

OPEN DURING DAYLIGHT HOURS

Church of Scotland **A**

301 ST MARY'S CHURCH, ESKADALE

A spacious white harled church in a picturesque woodland setting. Built 1826 by the 14th Lord Lovat. Alterations and additions by Peter Paul Pugin, 1881. Founder's tomb in the chancel. Lovat family graveyard to the west of the church. The stable, 50 metres to the west of the church is an unusual feature. On a minor road on the south east side of the River Beauly (OS453399). Served by St Mary's, Beauly. Sunday Mass 1pm

OPEN BY ARRANGEMENT

Contact Mr James Christie tel 01463 741536

Roman Catholic **B**

302 FEARN ABBEY NH837773

Fearn

Known as 'The Lamp of the North', it is one of the oldest pre-Reformation Scottish churches still in use for worship. Rebuilt 1772 by James Rich and restored by Ian G. Lindsay & Partners, 1972. Originally a monastery of Premonstratensian monks of the Order of St Augustine. Patrick Hamilton, burnt for heresy at St Andrews in 1528, was the Commendatory Abbot from 1517 to 1528. A9, Hill of Fearn Village. Sunday Service 11am

OPEN MAY–SEPTEMBER SATURDAY & SUNDAY 10AM–4.30PM

Or by appointment contact Mr B. Paterson tel 01862 832756

Church of Scotland A

Fearn Abbey

303 ST BENEDICT'S ABBEY CHURCH, FORT AUGUSTUS NH3709

Victorian monastery on the site and incorporating substantial parts of a Hanoverian fortress built to command the narrow centre of the Great Glen. The conversion to Gothic abbey was begun in 1876 by the architect Joseph A. Hansom who altered the fort buildings to provide a monastery, school and guest house. The church, designed by Peter Paul Pugin, was started 1893, restarted 1914 with Reginald Fairlie as architect, and choir and nave completed 1956. In 1966 Charles W. Gray added the west narthex, baptistry and porch, and in 1980 an apse was added thus completing the church. The church reflects the changing architecural and liturgical fashions of the 90-year building period. with many interesting furnishings. Services weekdays, Morning Office 6am, Community Mass 9.15am, Midday Office 12.40pm, Vespers 6pm, Compline 8.20pm; Sundays as weekdays except Morning Office 7am and Parish Mass 11am. Inter-church Services several times a year, in Advent, during Church Unity Week and at Whitsun

OPEN WEEKDAYS 6AM–8.30PM, SUNDAYS 7AM–8.30PM

Guided tours in summer

Roman Catholic B

304 FORT GEORGE CHAPEL NH761567

Fort George, Ardersier, Inverness

The garrison chapel built in 1767, William Skinner. Interior, 2-tiered arcade on three sides supported by Roman Doric columns. 18th-century 3-decker pulpit. Working garrison. Visitor displays, Historic Scotland. Off A96, north-east of Inverness

OPEN APRIL–SEPTEMBER MONDAY TO SATURDAY 9.30AM–6.30PM, SUNDAY 2–6.30PM, OCTOBER–MARCH MONDAY TO SATURDAY 9.30AM–4.30PM, SUNDAY 2–4.30PM

Non-denominational A

305 GAIRLOCH FREE CHURCH NG804761
Gairloch

On a commanding site overlooking Loch Gairloch. Gothic in style, to a design by Matthews & Lawrie, 1881. Simple interior with original fittings and Gothic panelled gallery across east end. Spandrels of roof trusses with cusped decoration. Fabric appeal. A832 to Gairloch. Sunday Services 11am & 5pm

OPEN BY ARRANGEMENT
Contact the Minister tel 01445 712371
Free Church of Scotland **C**

306 ST MARY AND ST FINNAN CHURCH, GLENFINNAN

The church was consecrated in 1873. Designed by E. Welby Pugin in the Gothic style, the church enjoys an elevated and commanding position overlooking Loch Shiel with a spectacular view of the loch and surrounding hills. The church is a memorial chapel to the MacDonalds of Glenaladale, the family with whom Bonnie Prince Charlie stayed prior to the raising of the Jacobite standard at Glenfinnan in August 1745. The church contains memorial stones to the Prince and to members of the MacDonald family. In the village, 15 miles west of Fort William on A830 to Mallaig. Sunday Mass 1pm

OPEN DAILY SUNRISE TO SUNSET
Roman Catholic **B**

307 OLD HIGH CHURCH, INVERNESS NH6645
Church Street, Inverness

Present building completed 1772, to a plan by George Fraser of Edinburgh, on site of medieval church, traditionally on the site where St Columba converted Brude, King of the Picts to Christianity. Porches, apse and chancel arch date from 1891, to designs by Ross & Macbeth. Lowest portion of the west bell tower is 15th or 16th century. The colours of the Queen's Own Cameron Highlanders are hung and the Regiment's Books of Remembrance are housed in the church. 2-manual organ by Henry Willis & Sons, 1895, rebuilt by H. Hilsdon, 1923. Stained glass by, amongst others, Douglas Strachan, 1925, Stephen Adam & Co., 1893 and A. Ballantine & Gardiner, 1899. Sunday Service 11.15am all year, Fridays 1pm, June, July and August only

Old High Church, Inverness

OPEN JUNE, JULY & AUGUST FRIDAYS NOON–2PM
Guided tour at 12.30pm
Scottish Episcopal **A**

308 ST ANDREW'S CATHEDRAL, INVERNESS

Ardross Street, Inverness

First new Cathedral completed in Great Britain after the Reformation, 1869 by local architect Alexander Ross. Polished granite pillars, stained glass, fine furnishings. Angel font after Thorvaldsen. Founder's memorial, ikons presented by Tsar of Russia. Peal of bells. Fine choir. On west bank of River Ness, just above Ness Bridge, A862, close to town centre. Sunday Services Eucharist 8.15am, Family Eucharist 9.30am, Sung Eucharist 11am, Choral Evensong 6.30pm

OPEN DAILY 8.30AM–6PM (LATER JUNE–SEPTEMBER)

Scottish Episcopal May–Sept WC A

309 ST MARY'S CHURCH, INVERNESS

30 Huntly Street, Inverness

On the west bank of the River Ness, very close to the town centre, 1837 by William Robertson. Between pedestrian bridge and traffic bridge. Sunday Services Mass 10am & 6.30pm. Vigil Mass Saturday 7pm

OPEN DAILY SUMMER 8AM–9PM WINTER 9AM–5PM

Roman Catholic A

310 ST STEPHEN'S, INVERNESS

Southside Road, Inverness

By W.L. Carruthers, 1897, in Arts and Crafts Gothic, the hall added later. The church consists of a nave, single north transept and an apsidal chancel. Square tower with a delicate needle spire. High open roof, pulpit of locally grown native oak. Noteworthy stained glass of 1897 and 1906 by A. Ballantine & Son. 2-manual organ by Wadsworth Bros, 1902. At junction of Old Edinburgh Road and Southside Road. Sunday Service 10am, Evening Communion 8pm 4th Sunday of June and last Sunday of January, April and September

OPEN BY ARRANGEMENT

Contact the Minister tel 01463 237129

Church of Scotland WC B

311 LAIRG PARISH CHURCH

Church Hill Road, Lairg

A simple Gothic church, built of local granite,1847, by William Leslie, the architect of Dunrobin Castle. The graveyard, 1½ miles away, served the original church and contains some interesting monuments, including a large marble monument to Sir James Matheson of Achany. Linked with St Callan's, Rogart and Pitfure. Sunday Service 10.45am, also 6.30pm on 1st Sunday of month

OPEN BY ARRANGEMNT

Contact Revd J. Goskirk tel 01549 402373

Church of Scotland

312 LOCHCARRON PARISH CHURCH (WEST CHURCH) NG8939

Originally United Free Church. By Wiliam Mackenzie, 1910. Historic graveyard at entrance to village. Strathcarron railway station distant 3 miles. Services every Sunday 11am and 2nd and 4th Sunday 6pm

OPEN DURING DAYLIGHT HOURS

Church of Scotland (after services)

313 OUR LADY AND ST BEAN, MARYDALE

Simple stone church in Gothic style, with adjoining presbytery, walled garden, school and schoolhouse, built as a unit by Joseph A. Hansom, 1868. The church has nave and apse with a porch and circular bell tower. St Bean is said to have been a monk of Iona, a cousin of St Columba, and the first to evangelise Strathglass. Sputan Bhain (OS334305) was the spring at which he baptised, and on the other side of the road is Clachan Comair, a walled graveyard with the ruins of a small 16th–17th-century church, on the site of an early 10th-century chapel dedicated to St Bean. Served by St Mary's Beauly. Sunday Mass 9am On north side of A831, between Cannich Bridge and Comar Bridge

OPEN DAILY

Roman Catholic **B**

314 NAIRN OLD PARISH CHURCH NH8856

Academy Street/Inverness Road, Nairn

Considered the finest structure in the area, 1897 by John Starforth. Architecture of Early English Transition period, Gothic reminiscences are abundant. Transeptal in form but almost circular in shape. Square tower is almost 100-ft high. Lovely light interior. Glorious stained glass. Sunday Service 11am, also June–August 9.30am

OPEN WEEKDAYS 9.30AM–12.30PM

Church of Scotland **A**

315 ST MOLUAG, EORROPAIDH, NESS

The building probably dates from the 12th century, but the site is believed to have been consecrated in the 6th century and is probably the place where Christianity was first preached to the people of Lewis. The church was restored in 1912 by Norman Forbes of Stornoway, under the guidance of the architect J.S. Richardson; the altars and pulpit date from this restoration. The side chapel is connected to the main church only through a squint. The church has no heating, electricity or water; lighting is by candles and oil lamps. 200 yards from B8013 (signed Eorropaidh from A857). Services 11am Easter Day and on first Sunday of May–September

OPEN DURING DAYLIGHT HOURS EASTER TO 1ST SUNDAY IN SEPTEMBER

Vehicular access impossible. In wet weather path to church can be muddy

Scottish Episcopal **A**

316 PITFURE CHURCH

Pitfure

A simple, pleasant place to worship. Built by the United Free congregation, 1910. Linked with Lairg and St Callan's Rogart. Sunday Service 1st, 3rd & 5th Sundays of month, October–May 12.15pm, June–Septemeber 11.30am

OPEN DAILY

Church of Scotland

317 ST CALLAN'S CHURCH, ROGART

Rebuilt in 1777 on the site of a medieval church. The austere whitewashed exterior, with its plain sash windows gives little hint of the warm, gleaming interior. A high canopied pulpit stands against the east wall. Long communion table and pews. Other pews are tiered from the entrance to the west end. Two small stained glass memorial windows on either side of the pulpit, Nativity and Penitence by Margaret Chilton and Marjorie Kemp, 1929. Modern vestry wing built in 1984.

From crossroads at Pittentrail, take Rhilochan/Balnacoil road. Church on right approx 2 miles. Linked with Lairg and Pitfure. Sunday Service 2nd and 4th Sundays of month, October–May 12.15pm, June–September 1.30pm

OPEN DAILY

Church of Scotland WC B

318 ST JOHN THE BAPTIST CHURCH, ROTHIEMURCHUS

Rothiemurchus

Church founded by John Peter Grant, 11th Laird of Rothiemurchus, 1930 by Sir Ninian Comper. A simple white interior with a groin vaulted ceiling and a rose damask baldacchino. Simple burial ground surrounds the church. Approximately 1 mile from the centre of Aviemore, 'the little white church on the ski road'. Sunday Service Holy Eucharist 10.30am

OPEN DAY SATURDAY 20 JUNE 2–5PM

Scottish Episcopal B

319 ST PETER'S & ST ANDREW'S CHURCH, THURSO ND115684

Princes Street, Thurso

Built in 1832 to a design by William Burn, the church is the centre point of the town, fronted by town square garden and war memorial. U-plan gallery. Pipe organ, Norman & Beard, 1914. Stained glass includes 'The Sower' by Oscar Paterson, 1922. Sunday Services 11am & 6.30pm

OPEN JULY–AUGUST DAILY 2–4PM 7–8PM

Church of Scotland WC B

St Peter's & St Andrew's Church, Thurso

· Inverclyde ·

320 ST NINIAN'S CHURCH, GOUROCK

18 Royal Street, Gourock

Gourock formed part of the pre-Reformation parish of Inverkip, mentioned in Papal registers of 1216–27. In 1878 Archbishop Eyre of Glasgow arranged for the construction of a chapel-school to be dedicated to St Ninian. The foundation stone was laid in 1879. Extension carried out in 1982 for the visit to Scotland of Pope John Paul II. The altar contains marble from the papal altar at Bellahouston. Mosaics by Frank Tritschler, stained glass by Dom Ninian Sloan of Pluscarden Abbey, and a chasuble fashioned from an original Paisley shawl by Debbie Gonet. Small museum. Sunday Mass 9.30am & 11.30am, Daily 10am & Vigil Mass Saturday 5.30pm

OPEN DAILY 9AM–4PM

Contact parish Priests for access to museum tel 01475 632078

Roman Catholic WC

321 KILMACOLM OLD KIRK NS3567

Kilmacolm

Built in 1830, James Dempster, Greenock, on the site of 13th and 16th-century churches. 13th-century chancel is incorporated as the Murray Chapel. South aisle, J.B. Wilson, Glasgow, added 1903, contains stained glass window by C.E. Moira. Other stained glass by Norman Macdougall. Near centre of village, west of junction of B786 with A761. Sunday Service 11am, July & August 10am

OPEN DAILY 10AM–4PM

Church of Scotland WC **B**

· North Lanarkshire ·

322 NEW MONKLAND PARISH CHURCH, AIRDRIE

Condorrat Road, Glenmavis, Airdrie

A fine old Scots plain kirk which hides an attractive interior, Andrew Bell of Airdrie, 1776. It holds a commanding position at the highest point in the village, and incorporates the bell tower of an earlier church (1698) which housed a cell for minor offenders The old church was replaced when it "suffered so badly from overcrowding that youthful members of the congregation colonised the exposed joists to roost!" The apse was added in 1904 by John Arthur. Extensive restoration 1997. Simple watchhouse by the cemetery and a number of interesting grave stones. Sunday Service 11am

OPEN BY ARRANGEMENT

Contact Mr John Blades tel 01236 766511

Church of Scotland WC **B**

323 OVERTOWN PARISH CHURCH
Main Street, Overtown, by Wishaw
Village church built in 1876. Near picturesque Clyde Valley, Strathclyde Country Park and many other places of interest. A71, Edinburgh to Kilmarnock, 35 miles from Edinburgh
OPEN 9TH & 16TH MAY FOR SALE OF PLANTS, WITH GUIDED TOURS AND CAFE
Church of Scotland

324 STEPPS PARISH CHURCH NS6568
17 Whitehill Avenue, Stepps
Fine example of the neo-Gothic style favoured by ecclesiastical architect P. MacGregor Chalmers, 1900. Designed to reflect scale and simplicity of a village church. Interesting stained glass. Pipe organ, Joseph Brook 1884, rebuilt James MacKenzie 1976. On rail and bus routes Glasgow–Cumbernauld. Sunday Service 10am mid–June–mid–August, 11am mid–August–mid–June
OPEN TUESDAY AND THURSDAY 10AM–12 NOON ALL YEAR
Other times tel 0141 779 2504
Church of Scotland

· South Lanarkshire ·

325 BIGGAR KIRK NT0437
Kirkstyle, Biggar
Rebuilt 1546, the last collegiate church to be formed before the Reformation in Scotland. A cruciform building with fine stained glass, including work by William Wilson and Crear McCartney. In the kirkyard are memorials to William Ewart Gladstone and Thomas Blackwood Murray, the Scottish motor pioneer of 'Albion'. From M74, A702, 12 miles from Abington. Sunday Services 11am also 9.30am June, July & August
OPEN DAILY IN SUMMER 9AM–5PM
In winter key from Moat Park Heritage Centre opposite
Church of Scotland **B**

326 BOTHWELL PARISH CHURCH NS7058
Main Street, Bothwell
Scotland's oldest Collegiate Church still in use for worship and dedicated to St Bride, occupies the site of a former 6th-century church. Medieval choir. Nave and tower 1833, David Hamilton, altered 1933. Monuments to the Earls of Douglas and the Duke of Hamilton. Stained glass by Gordon Webster, Douglas Strachan and Sir Edward Burne-Jones. Fascinating tales of an outstanding royal wedding and link with Bothwell Castle. Graveyard. Off A725 near Hamilton. Sunday Service 10.30am
OPEN DAILY EASTER–SEPTEMBER
Bus parties welcome by arrangement tel 01698 853189
Church of Scotland WC **A**

327 CAMBUSLANG OLD PARISH CHURCH

3 Cairns Road, Kirkhill, Cambuslang

St Cadoc is believed to have had a holy site here *c* 550AD, and early buildings have been recorded from 12th century. The present building is by David Cousin, 1841. Steeple with clock and bell. The chancel is by P. MacGregor Chalmers, 1922. Stained glass and tapestries by Sadie McLennan 1957. Heraldic shields of heritors decorate the ceiling. Interesting gravestones in churchyard including one to Revd William McCulloch, Minister at Scotland's largest ever revival 'The Cambuslang Wark' in 1742. Near Greenlees Road B759. Sunday Service September–June 11am & 6.30pm, July & August 9.30am & 11am

OPEN BY ARRANGEMENT

Contact Mr A. Smith tel 0141 641 3585

Church of Scotland WC **B**

328 DALSERF PARISH CHURCH NS7950

Dalserf

Built 1655, centre transept added 1892. Oblong building with pulpit on long side. Outside stairs to three galleries. Belfry. The graveyard contains a pre-Norman hogback stone and an outstanding covenanting memorial, 1753, to Revd John MacMillan, founder of the Reformed Presbyterian Church. Off A72 between Garrion Bridge and Rosebank. Sunday Service 12 noon

OPEN BY ARRANGEMENT

Contact Church Officer Mr W. Knox tel 01698 883770

Church of Scotland WC **A**

Dalserf Parish Church

329 DRUMCLOG MEMORIAL KIRK NS6438

Drumclog

1912 by J. McLellan Fairley. The church has strong associations with the covenanters. A71, 5 miles west on Darvel road. Linked with Avendale Old Church. Sunday Service 9.30am

OPEN BY ARRANGEMENT

Contact Mr J. Spence tel 01357 521939

Church of Scotland

330 GLASSFORD PARISH CHURCH NS7247

Jackson Street, Glassford

Built 1820. Memorial stained glass windows to Revd Gavin Lang, grandfather of Cosmo Lang, Archbishop of Canterbury. Ruins of 1633 church and covenanter's stone. Off A71 Stonehouse–Strathaven or A723 Hamilton–Strathaven. Linked with Strathaven East. Sunday Service 10am

OPEN BY ARRANGEMENT

Also Doors Open Day. Contact Revd W. Stewart tel 01357 521138

Church of Scotland WC **B**

331 HAMILTON OLD PARISH CHURCH NS7255

Strathmore Road, Hamilton

Georgian gem, designed and built by William Adam, 1734. Samples from the roof timbers found to be full of lead shot – Adam used wood from an old Man of War! Chancel furnishings include embroidery by Hannah Frew Paterson. Exceptionally detailed engraved glass windows by Anita Pate depict the history of the church. Memorial stained glass window of African animals to John Stevenson Hamilton, founder of Kruger National Park. 11th-century Netherton Cross and covenanting memorials in graveyard. In centre of town. Sunday Service 10.45am, July & August 10am

OPEN MONDAY TO FRIDAY 10.30AM–3.30PM

Or by arrangement tel 01698 281905 Monday–Friday 9am–1pm

Easter Sunday church decorated with thousands of daffodils

Church of Scotland (by arrangement) WC **A**

332 ST NICHOLAS PARISH CHURCH, LANARK NS8843

The Cross, Lanark

By John Reid of Nemphlar, 1774. Stained glass, baptismal font in Caen stone. Fine pipe organ. On A73, 30 miles south of Glasgow, follow signs for New Lanark. Sunday Service 11am, Wednesday 10.15am

OPEN DOORS OPEN DAY AND BY ARRANGEMENT

Contact Revd J. Thomson tel 01555 662600.

Kirkin' of Lord Cornet 2 June 12 noon

Church of Scotland WC **B**

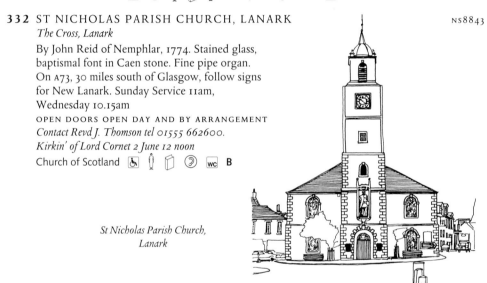

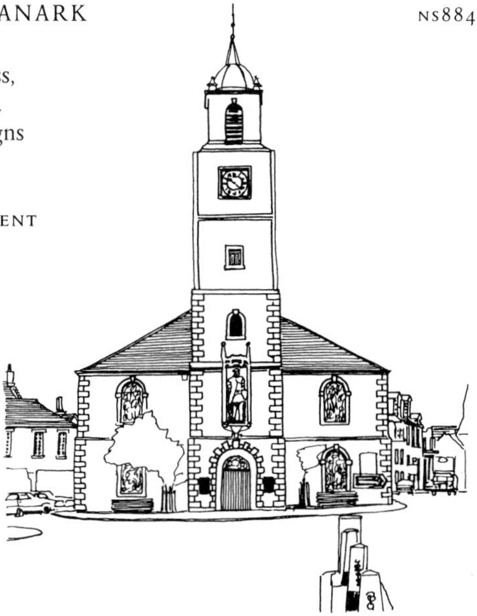

St Nicholas Parish Church, Lanark

333 LESMAHAGOW OLD PARISH CHURCH

David I granted a church and lands to the Tironensian monks in 1144. He also granted the right of sanctuary, violated in 1335 when the church was burned, with villagers inside, by John Eltham brother of Edward I. The present church was built in 1803 and the apse added in the 1890s. Pipe organ, 1889. Several stained glass windows including one whose central panel, 'The Descent from the Cross', is a copy of that in Antwerp cathedral. The bell is dated 1625. Display in the Chapter House. Lesmahagow on M74, 23 miles south of Glasgow. A conservation village. Sunday Service 11am

OPEN BY ARRANGEMENT

Contact Revd Sheila Mitchell tel 01555 892425

Church of Scotland

334 RUTHERGLEN OLD PARISH CHURCH

Main Street x Queen Street, Rutherglen

The present church was designed by the architect J.J. Burnet, 1902, in Gothic style, the fourth on this site since the original foundation in the 6th century. The gable end of an 11th-century church still stands in the graveyard supporting St Mary's steeple (15th century). It contains the church bell, 1635. Stained glass including a Word War I memorial. Communion cups dated 1665 are still in use. The churchyard occupies an ancient site, at its gateway two stone offertory shelters and a sundial set above its entrance dated 1679. Sunday Service 11am

OPEN 2ND SATURDAY OF EVERY MONTH 10AM–12 NOON

Church of Scotland WC B

335 ST COLUMBKILLE'S CHURCH, RUTHERGLEN NS6161

Main Street, Rutherglen

Magnificent church by Coia, 1940, replacing original church founded in 1851. A modern adaptation of an Italian basilica. Between A724 and A731. Trains and city buses. Sunday Masses 9am, 10.30am, 12 noon & 7pm; Vigil Mass Saturday 5.30pm

OPEN MONDAY TO THURSDAY 9AM–5PM FRIDAY 9AM–2PM

Roman Catholic WC

336 AVENDALE OLD PARISH CHURCH, STRATHAVEN NS7044

59a Kirk Street, Strathaven

Records show a church in Strathaven in 1288. This church was built in 1772 and the interior renovated 1879. The centre section of the south gallery was reserved for the family and tenants of the Duke of Hamilton and is known as 'The Duke's Gallery'. Stained glass window of the Last Supper, Crear McCartney, 1996. In town centre A71. Sunday Service 11am, also 1st and 3rd Sundays except January, June & August 7pm

OPEN MONDAY TO FRIDAY 9AM–12 NOON (NOT SCHOOL HOLIDAYS)

Other times contact Session Clerk tel 01357 521939

Church of Scotland WC B

Avendale Old Parish Church, Strathaven

337 STRATHAVEN EAST PARISH CHURCH

Green Street, Strathaven

The white painted exterior is a local landmark. Built 1777 with clock tower added 1843. Major rebuilding 1877. Prominent pulpit and memorial windows. Linked with Glassford Church. Sunday Service 11.30am

OPEN BY ARRANGEMENT

Contact Revd W. Stewart tel 01357 521138

Church of Scotland WC **A** (tower) **B** (church)

· East Lothian ·

Local Representative: Mrs Margaret Beveridge
St Andrew's, Duns Road, Gifford EH41 4QW

338 ABERLADY PARISH CHURCH NT462798

Main Street, Aberlady

15th-century tower, the body of the church recast in 1886 by William Young. Stained glass by Edward Frampton, London,1889. 8th-century cross. Marble monument attributed to Canova. Tour guide boards in English, French, German, Spanish, Swedish. A198 Edinburgh–North Berwick. Sunday Service 11.15am

OPEN 1 MAY–30 SEPTEMBER 10AM–DUSK

Other times contact Dr Hutchison tel 01875 870413 or J. Wood tel 01875 870704

Guides and sales June, July & August, Saturday & Sunday 2.30–5pm

Church of Scotland A

339 ATHELSTANEFORD PARISH CHURCH NT533774

Athelstaneford

The original church 'Ecclesia de Elstaneford' on this site is said to have been founded in 1176 by the Countess Ada, mother of William the Lion. The present church dates from 1780. Cruciform design with central aisle, transepts and semi-octagonal chancel. Bellcote on the west gable. Three stained glass windows by C.E. Kempe. Doocot, 1583. Church has historic link with the Scottish Saltire: commemorative plaque and Saltire floodlit. Heritage Centre to rear of church opened in 1997 with audio visual display (entry free) From A1, B1347. Sunday Service 10am

OPEN DAILY DAWN TO DUSK

Church of Scotland B

340 BOLTON PARISH CHURCH NT507701

Bolton

There has been a church on this site since before 1244. The present building dates from 1809 and remains structurally unchanged since that time. The architect was probably Archibald Elliot. The interior is plain and unspoiled, complete with Carpenter's Gothic pulpit and gallery on clustered iron posts. Robert Burns's mother, brother and sisters are buried in the churchyard. Graveguard and other items dating from the time of the 'Resurrection Men' displayed in the porch. Linked with Saltoun, Humbie and Yester. B6368 from Haddington. Sunday Service 10am, alternating with Saltoun

OPEN DAILY

Church of Scotland B

341 COCKENZIE METHODIST CHURCH NT398756

28 Edinburgh Road, Cockenzie

The third of East Lothian's three Primitive Methodist Chapels, 1878. Simple and attractive. Original interior. South side of main road at west end of village. Sunday Service 2.30pm

OPEN BY ARRANGEMENT

Contact church office tel 01875 610388

Methodist

342 DIRLETON KIRK NT5184

Dirleton

Attractive stone building erected in 1612 to replace 12th-century kirk in Gullane which was 'continewallie overblawin with sand'. Archerfield Aisle added 1650, first example of neo-classical design in Scotland. Tower crowned with Gothic pinnacles, 1836. Stained glass window depicting St Francis and the Animals, Margaret Chilton 1936. Sunday Service 11.45am, and 8–8.30pm July & August

OPEN DAILY 10AM–DUSK

Light lunches, snacks in Dirleton Gallery adjacent

Church of Scotland A

Dirleton Kirk

343 DUNBAR METHODIST CHURCH NT6778

10 Victoria Street, Dunbar

Scotland's oldest Methodist Church, built in 1764. John and Charles Wesley were trustees and John often preached here. Enlarged 1857, renovated 1890. Fine interior, unexpected from plain exterior. Oak pulpit. Stained glass windows from St Giles Cathedral, Edinburgh. South side of road leading from High Street to Harbour. Sunday Service 11am

OPEN ON LIFEBOAT DAY (LATE JULY)

Contact church office tel 01875 610388

Methodist A

344 DUNBAR PARISH CHURCH

Queen's Road, Dunbar

The building, designed by Gillespie Graham in 1821, has been beautifully reconstructed by Campbell & Arnott 1990, following a devastating fire in 1987. The colourful and modern interior includes the early 17th-century monument to the Earl of Dunbar and some fine stained glass by Shona McInnes and Douglas Hogg 1990. 200 yards south of High Street south end. Intercity trains to Dunbar. Sunday Service 11am

OPEN JUNE–MID SEPTEMBER MONDAY TO FRIDAY 11AM–4PM

Church of Scotland A

345 ST ANNE'S CHURCH, DUNBAR

Westgate, Dunbar

The church is by H.M. Wardrop and Sir R. Rowand Anderson, 1890. Built in the Gothic revival style and decorated with some Scots detail. Carved oak furnishings, Henry Willis organ, stained glass by Ballantine & Gardiner, Heaton, Butler & Bayne and the Abbey Studio. North end of Dunbar High Street. Sunday Service 11am

OPEN SATURDAY 20 JUNE10AM–4PM

Other times contact Revd G. Grunnevald tel 01368 865711

Scottish Episcopal (open day only) **B**

346 PRESTONKIRK PARISH CHURCH, EAST LINTON NT5977

Preston Road, East Linton

Dedicated to St Baldred, the church possesses in its former chancel the best fragment of 13th-century church architecture in East Lothian. The tower dates from 1631, the main building from 1770, enlarged 1824, redesigned internally 1892 by James Jerdan. Organ by Vincent of Sutherland. St Baldred window 1959 and two World War II memorial windows by William Wilson. Among the gravestones are those of Andrew Meikle, inventor of the threshing machine, and George Rennie, agriculturalist and brother of John Rennie, the civil engineer. Off A1, follow signs to Preston Mill. Sunday Service 11.30am, Ecumenical Service last Sunday of month 6pm

OPEN JUNE–AUGUST SUNDAY 2–4PM

Other times tel the Minister 01620 8605227

Church of Scotland **A**

347 SALTOUN PARISH CHURCH, EAST SALTOUN NT475679

East Saltoun

Ther has been a church on this site since before 1244. The present building is a T-plan Gothic kirk of 1805, John Fletcher Campbell, built 'as a monument to the virtues of his ancestors'. The actual designer is most likely to have been Robert Burn. The interior was recast in 1885, the architect was John Lessels. Beneath the church lies the Fletcher Vault, containing the remains of Andrew Fletcher 'The Patriot' and members of his family. Linked with Bolton, Humbie and Yester. Sunday Service 10am alternating with Bolton

OPEN DAILY

Church of Scotland **A**

348 YESTER PARISH CHURCH, GIFFORD NT535682

Main Street, Gifford

By James Smith, finished 1710. A white harled T-plan church with square staged tower and slated spire. Weather vane in the form of a heron, William Brown, Edinburgh 1709. Church bell, from the old Church of Bothans, 1492. Pulpit 17th century with bracket for baptismal basin. Memorial in village wall opposite to Revd John Witherspoon, son of the Manse, signed the American Declaration of Independence 1784. B6369 from Haddington. Hourly bus service. Sunday Service 11.30am

OPEN DAILY APRIL–OCTOBER 9AM–SUNSET

Village gala day June, flower show August

Church of Scotland **A**

349 GULLANE PARISH CHURCH (ST ANDREW'S) NT4882
East Links Road, Gullane

The church,designed by Glasgow architect John Honeyman and completed in 1888, replaced an earlier 12th-century building vacated in 1612 when the congregation was rehoused in a new kirk at Dirleton. The Kirk Session of Dirleton decided to build the present parish church for the benefit of 'the large number of summer visitors annually residing in the village'. Simple Norman style with east apse. The zigzagged chancel arch is derived from the old parish church, as is the south doorway whose tympanum has a low relief of St Andrew. A198 to North Berwick. Sunday Service 9.45am

OPEN DAILY ALL YEAR
Coffee Tuesdays 10–11.30am
Church of Scotland [♿] [👤] [⌂] [♫] **A**

350 ST ADRIAN'S, GULLANE
Sandy Loan, Gullane

A simple aisleless church in Arts and Crafts style by Reginald Fairlie, 1926. Built of stone from the Rattlebag quarry, with a low tower and slated pyramidal spire. 3-light chancel window by Douglas Strachan, 1934. Sandy Loan is first right going westwards from Queen's Hotel. Sunday Services 9.30 Sung Eucharist, Said Eucharist 1st & 3rd Sundays 8am

OPEN 10AM–5PM APRIL–SEPTEMBER
Coffee Tuesdays 10–11.30am
Scottish Episcopal [♿] [♫] [⌂] **B**

351 HOLY TRINITY CHURCH, HADDINGTON NT5173
Church Street, Haddington

Built 1770 on site of original 'Lamp of Lothian'. Chancel added, 1930. Stations of the Cross, Bowman. Christ Crucified, Sutherland. Lord Wemyss' breakfast room (off former gallery). Medieval walls of former priory and town defences. Sunday Services 8.30am, 10am Eucharist, Wednesday 10am Eucharist

OPEN WEDNESDAY 10AM–4PM AND IN SUMMER SATURDAY 10AM–4PM
Other times contact the Rectory adjacent
Scottish Episcopal [♿] [👤] [☐] [⌂] [♫] [wc] **B**

352 ST MARY'S COLLEGIATE CHURCH, HADDINGTON NT518736
Sidegate, Haddington

Dating back to the 14th century, one of the three great pre-Reformation churches of the Lothians. Known as 'The Lamp of Lothian', largest parish church in Scotland with fascinating history. Nave, repaired for John Knox and the reformers after siege of Haddington 1548, and used as the parish church for almost 400 years. Transepts and choir restored, Ian G. Lindsay & Partners, 1973. Lauderdale Aisle, now The Chapel of the Three Kings, in regular ecumenical use. Fine stone carvings, especially west door. Notable stained glass. Modern tapestries. Fine pipe organ by Lammermuir Pipe Organs, 1990. Sunday Services 9.30am Family Circle and 11am

OPEN 1 APRIL–30 SEPTEMBER DAILY 11AM–4.30PM, SUNDAY 2–4.30PM
Annual ecumenical Haddington/Whitekirk Pilgrimage Saturday 9 May. Brass Rubbing Centre open Saturday throughout season 1–4pm except weddings
Church of Scotland [♿] [♫] [👤] [⌂] [☐] [👤] [☕] [wc] **A**

353 HUMBIE KIRK NT4662

Humbie

On the site of a pre-Reformation church, set in an ox-bow of Humbie Burn, a T-plan Gothic church by James Tod dated 1800. Vestry added 1846, and alterations by David Bryce, 1866. The chancel added 1930, probably W.J. Walker Todd. Open scissor-braced timber roof. Stained glass. Organ by David Hamilton, *c* 1840 with decorative Gothic dark wood case, from the Norwegian Seamen's Chapel at Granton. Fine gravestones with classical detail dating from earlier church. Broun Aisle, 1864, Bryce, sited at west gate, erected by Archibald Broun of Johnstonburn 'in lieu of the burial place of his family within the church, which in deference to the feelings of the parishioners, he has now closed'! Linked with Bolton, Saltoun and Yester. Sunday Service 10am

OPEN DAILY

Church of Scotland **B**

354 PARISH CHURCH OF ST MICHAEL'S, INVERESK NT344721

Musselburgh

There has been a church on the site since the 6th century. The present church was built in 1805 to the design of Robert Nisbet, the steeple by William Sibbald. The interior was reorientated and remodelled in 1893 by J. MacIntyre Henry. Known as the "visible Kirk" because of its prominent position, it stands on the site of a Roman praetorium and replaces a medieval church. Fine Adam-style ceiling and some excellent stained glass. Magnificent pipe organ enlarged, 1897 by Lewis & Co. of London. Surrounded by a fine graveyard with many interesting old stones. Sunday Service 11am

OPEN BY ARRANGEMENT

Contact Mr G. Burnet tel 0131 665 2689

Open when village gardens open under Scotland's Gardens Scheme

Church of Scotland ♿ (two steps to door) WC **A**

St Mary's Collegiate Church, Haddington

355 MUSSELBURGH CONGREGATIONAL CHURCH NT3472

6 Links Street, Musselburgh

Simple but charming Georgian building completed in 1801, built with stone carried by fishermen and sailors from the shores of the Forth at Fisherrow. Oldest church in Musselburgh and one of first Congregational churches in Scotland. Pipe organ, fine example of the work of George Holdich, built 1860 for St Michael's, Appleby. Rebuilt for Musselburgh Congregational church, 1977. Church sits behind Brunton Hall. Sunday Service 11am

OPEN 20–27 SEPTEMBER AND BY ARRANGEMENT

200th Anniversary celebrations Service of Dedication 20 September 11am, Service of Rededication Sunday 27 September 11am. Many events during this week

Contact Mr J. Brown, 11 Links Street tel 0131 665 3768

Congregational WC C

356 ABBEY CHURCH, NORTH BERWICK NT5485

High Street, North Berwick

Built 1868 as United Presbyterian by Robert R. Raeburn in Early English style. A complete early 20th-century scheme of stained glass with, superimposed on one window, an arrangement of suspended planes representing an ascent of doves, by Sax Shaw, 1972. Sunday Services 10.15am & 6pm

OPEN 9AM–6PM MONDAYS–FRIDAYS JULY & AUGUST

Church of Scotland WC

357 ST BALDRED'S CHURCH, NORTH BERWICK

Dirleton Avenue, North Berwick

The original church by John Henderson, 1861, was cleverly extended in 1863 incorporating the old masonry by Seymour & Kinross, who also designed the altar. The porch with its magnificent carved doors was added by Robert Lorimer in 1916. Choir stalls by H.O. Tarbolton, porch doors by Mrs Meredith-Williams. Stained glass by Ballantine & Son. Convenient for North Berwick railway station. Services every Sunday Sung Eucharist 11am, 2nd & 4th Sunday Said Eucharist 8am

OPEN ALL YEAR 10AM–4PM

Scottish Episcopal B

Musselburgh Congregational Church

358 PENCAITLAND PARISH CHURCH NT4468

Consecrated in 1242, the earliest part of the church dates from the 12th century. The present building consists of nave, with a gallery at the west end, and two aisles on the north side, the older called the Winton Aisle and the other the Saltoun Aisle. Churchyard with many interesting gravestones, offering houses, renovated carriage house, stables, harness room and cottage. A1 from Edinburgh to Tranent, B6355 to Pencaitland. Bus 113 from Edinburgh. Sunday Service 10am, 3rd Sunday 'Face-to-Face' celebration 6.30pm in the Carriage House, last Sunday Healing Service 6.30pm in the Winton Aisle

OPEN JULY & AUGUST SUNDAY 2–5PM,
SEPTEMBER TO JUNE SATURDAY 9.30AM–1PM

Other times contact Revd C. Donaldson tel 01875 340208

Church of Scotland A

Pencaitland Parish Church

359 CHALMERS MEMORIAL CHURCH, PORT SETON

Edinburgh Road, Port Seton

Built to a design by Sydney Mitchell for the United Free Church, the foundation stone was laid in 1904. It has a very elegant spire and bell tower and unique stencilled interior. Stained glass windows by Margaret Chilton and Marjorie Kemp, 1924–50. Sunday Service 11am

OPEN EASTER TO END SEPTEMBER WEDNESDAY AND SUNDAY 2–4PM

Church of Scotland A

360 STENTON PARISH CHURCH NT6274

Main Street. Stenton

By William Burn, 1829, a T-plan kirk with a splendid east tower. Redesigned internally by James Jerdan in 1892. Stained glass by C.E. Kempe and Ballantine & Gardiner. In the graveyard is a fragment of the 16th-century kirk and a fine selection of monuments. Rood well in village. Follow signs to Stenton off A1. Sunday Service 10am 2nd and 4th Sundays

OPEN DAILY DAWN TO DUSK

Church of Scotland B

361 TRANENT METHODIST CHURCH NT4072

63 Bridge Street, Tranent

Built 1870, second of East Lothian's three Primitive Methodist Chapels. Subdivided 1958 to create church hall. Simple interior. Monument to Barnabas Wild, minister 1890s. North side of main road at west end of town. Sunday Service 11am

OPEN 1ST SATURDAY OF MONTH FOR COFFEE MORNING

Methodist A

362 ST MARY'S PARISH CHURCH, WHITEKIRK NT5981
Whitekirk

Dating from 12th century, the original building was reconstructed during the 15th century starting with the vaulted stone choir, built in 1439 by Adam Hepburn of Hailes. In medieval times Whitekirk was an important place of pilgrimage. The church was set on fire in 1914 by suffragettes. Restored by Robert Lorimer. Ceiled wagon roof over nave and transepts, communion table, pulpit, lectern and font all by Lorimer. Stained glass by C.E. Kempe 1889 and Karl Parsons 1916. Tithe barn and historic graveyard. On A198. Sunday Service 11.30am

OPEN DAILY DAWN TO DUSK

Church of Scotland WC A

363 WHITTINGEHAME PARISH CHURCH NT6073
Main Street, Stenton

Spiky battlemented Gothic T-plan church built 1722, and added to by Barclay and Lamb in 1820 for James Balfour, grandfather of A.J. Balfour, Prime Minister 1902–05. 18th-century burial enclosure of Buchan Sydserfs of Ruchlaw and good late 17th-century headstones show that there was an earlier church on the site. Follow signs to Whittingehame off A1. Sunday Service 10am 1st and 3rd Sundays

OPEN JUNE–AUGUST SUNDAY 2–4PM

Church of Scotland B

· Midlothian ·

364 CRICHTON COLLEGIATE CHURCH NT381616
Crichton, Pathhead

Collegiate church rebuilt in 1440 by William Crichton, Lord Chancellor of Scotland. Restored by Hardy & White 1898. Present restoration by Benjamin Tindall. Fine pointed barrel vaults over choir and transepts and splendid square tower over crossing. Organ by Joseph Brook & Co. Magnificent position at head of Tyne valley close to Crichton Castle. Signed road B6367 from A68 at Pathhead. Evening Services 6.30pm on 26 April & 28 June. Remembrance Service 11 November 10.30am

OPEN MAY–SEPTEMBER SUNDAY 2–5PM OR BY APPOINTMENT

Contact tel 01875 320341 or 320364 for information about concerts or events
Crichton Castle open 1 April–30 September

Non-denominational WC A

Chrichton Collegiate Church

365 ST MARY'S CHURCH, DALKEITH NT335677
Dalkeith Country Park, Dalkeith
Built as the chapel for Dalkeith Palace in 1843 by William Burn and David Bryce. Early
English style with splendid features: double hammerbeam roof, heraldic floor tiles by
Minton, and the only working water-powered Hamilton organ in Scotland. Sunday Service
9.45am
OPEN MAY–SEPTEMBER SATURDAY & SUNDAY 2–5PM
Also teas & crafts July & August weekends. Summer concerts. Fun Day in September. For information tel
0131 663 3165
Scottish Episcopal [♿] 〖 ☐ ⊇ [wc] A

366 ST NICHOLAS BUCCLEUCH PARISH CHURCH, DALKEITH
High Street, Dalkeith
Medieval church, became collegiate in 1406. Nave and transepts 1854 by David Bryce. James,
1st Earl of Morton and his wife Princess Joanna (the profoundly deaf 3rd daughter of James I)
are buried within the choir, *c* 1498. Memorial monument with their effigies mark the burial
site. 200yds east of A68/A6094 junction. Sunday Services 9.30am Family worship, 11am
Parish worship
OPEN EASTER SUNDAY TO 30 SEPTEMBER WEEKDAYS 10AM–12 NOON & 2–4PM, SUNDAY
10–11AM
Or contact Mr A. Brown tel 0131 663 0799
Flower festival 8 & 9 June 12 noon –5pm
Church of Scotland [♿] ⑨ 〖 ⌂ ☐ ⌁ ⊇ [wc] A

367 PENICUIK SOUTH CHURCH NT2359
Peebles Road, Penicuik
Built 1863, F.T. Pilkington. Open timber roof.
Stained glass. Fully restored 1991. Short history
available, models of church on sale. Sunday
Services 11.15am & 7pm
OPEN SATURDAYS ALL YEAR 10AM–12 NOON
Church of Scotland [♿] ⌂ ⑨ ⌂ [wc] B

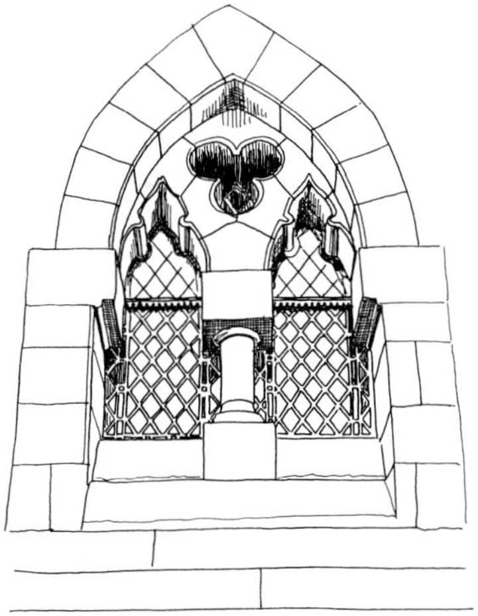

Penicuik South Church

368 ST JAMES THE LESS, PENICUIK
Broomhill Road, Penicuik

The original church, which now forms the nave, was designed by H. Seymour of Seymour & Kinross, 1882. The chancel, vestries, tower and bell were added by H.O. Tarbolton, 1899. An excellent lot of stained glass including one light by Shrigley & Hunt of Lancaster and four magnificent lights by C.E. Kempe. Rood screen designed by Tarbolton and carved by T. Good, communion rails also designed by Tarbolton and carved by Scott Morton & Co. Reredos designed and executed by Mrs Meredith-Williams, 1921. Services every Sunday 8 & 10.15am, 1st & 3rd Sundays Choral Evensong 6.30pm

OPEN BY ARRANGEMENT

Tel the Rector on 01968 672862

Scottish Episcopal WC B

369 ROSSLYN CHAPEL (ST MATTHEW'S) NT275631
Chapel Loan, Roslin

Built 1450 as the church of a college established by William Sinclair, third Earl of Orkney. Intended to be cruciform but only the choir was completed. Famous for its decorative stone carving that covers almost every part of the building. The 'Prentice Pillar' has spectacular decoration. Sunday Services 10.30am and 3.30pm (winter), 5.30pm (summer)

OPEN ALL YEAR MONDAY TO SATURDAY 10AM–5PM, SUNDAY 12 NOON–4.45PM

Scottish Episcopal WC A

· West Lothian ·

370 ST MICHAEL'S PARISH CHURCH, LINLITHGOW NS9977
Kirkgate, Linlithgow

One of the finest examples of a large medieval burgh church. Consecrated in 1242 on the site of an earlier church, most of the present building dates from the 15th century with some 19th-century restoration. Situated beside Linlithgow Palace, its history is intertwined with that of the Royal House of Stewart. The modern aluminium crown, 1964, symbolises the Church's continuing witness to Christ's Kingship. Window commemorating 750th anniversary of the church, 1992, by Crear McCartney. Peel tower, Linlithgow Palace and Loch adjacent. Sunday Services 9.30am & 11am

OPEN ALL YEAR MONDAY TO FRIDAY 10AM–12 NOON, 1.30–3.30PM

Church of Scotland (on request) A

371 LIVINGSTON VILLAGE KIRK NT0366
Kirk Lane, Livingston

There has been a church on the site since 12th century. The present building was rebuilt 1732. Late 18th-century pews and pulpit with Gothic sounding board and a pretty stair. Plaque in entrance commemorates covenanters from village drowned off Orkney. Kirkyard has some fine monuments from 17th and 18th centuries including some lively headstones featuring phoenixes and leafy cartouches. Close to Heritage Centre. Sunday Service 10am

OPEN BY ARRANGEMENT

Contact the Minister tel 01506 420227

Church of Scotland WC B

372 KIRK OF CALDER NT0767

Main Street, Mid Calder

This 16th-century parish church, recently restored, won the West Lothian Award for
Conservation in 1992. John Knox, James 'Paraffin' Young, David Livingston and Frederick
Chopin have already visited here – we look forward to meeting you too! Admission free,
donations welcome. 1995 restoration of stained glass windows. Off A71 on B7015 in village
of Mid Calder. LRT bus 9, SMT buses 26, 27, 285, 271, from Edinburgh. Sunday Service
10.30am

OPEN MAY–SEPTEMBER SUNDAY 2–4PM

Near to Almondell Country Park, open all year

Church of Scotland ♿ ⊘ 🕯 📖 ☕ WC A

Kirk of Calder

373 POLBETH HARWOOD PARISH CHURCH NT0767

Chapelton Drive, Polbeth, West Calder

The congregation was formed in 1795 and the church completed in 1796 as Burgher Kirk.
Congregation translated from West Calder to Polbeth 1962. A71 between Livingston New
Town and West Calder. 15 mins walk from West Calder station. Sunday Service 11am

OPEN MONDAY AND WEDNESDAY DURING SCHOOL TERM TIME 10AM–12 NOON,
THURSDAY 6–8PM DURING SUMMER

Church of Scotland ♿ ☕

374 TORPHICHEN KIRK

The Bowyett, Torphichen

Built in 1756 on the site of the nave of the 12th-century preceptory, it is a T-shaped building
with three galleries including a laird's loft. Two centre pews can be tipped back to form
extended communion tables. Sanctuary stone in the graveyard. Preceptory church adjoining
in the care of Historic Scotland; exhibition. Sunday Service 11.15am

OPEN PARISH CHURCH AND PRECEPTORY EASTER–END OCTOBER, SATURDAY 11AM–5PM,
SUNDAY 2–5PM

*Charge for entry to preceptory. Groups welcome for guided tours of both buildings. Contact Mrs Stirling
tel 01506 654142*

Church of Scotland 📖 🕯 ☐ WC A

· Moray ·

375 ST MARGARET OF SCOTLAND, ABERLOUR NJ2642

High Street, Aberlour

Designed by Alexander Ross and consecrated in 1879, the tall Gothic church retains its splendid original interior. Built for the orphanage 120 years ago, the feet of hundreds of children have worn down the Victorian tiled flooor. Lovely carvings of flowers, birds and squirrels on pillar capitals and screen arch. Sunday services 11am 1st Sunday in the month, 9.15am other Sundays

OPEN 1ST SATURDAY AUGUST 10AM–5PM. FLOWER FESTIVAL EARLY JUNE 10AM–5PM

Other times key from Aberlour Hotel – must be signed for

Scottish Episcopal A

376 ST PETER'S CHURCH, BUCKIE NJ4265

St Andrew's Square, Buckie

To plans donated by Bishop Kyle and supervised by Alexander Ellis of Elgin, opened 7 August 1857 on a site donated by Sir William Gordon. Rose window. High altar of Italian marble. Statue of St Margaret of Scotland, copy of original in Brussels. Saturday Vigil Mass 7.30pm, Sunday 10am, weekdays 9.30am

OPEN DAILY 9AM–6PM

Roman Catholic A

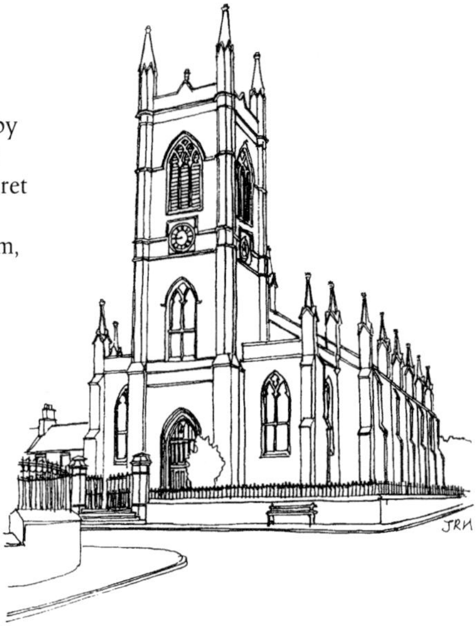

St Peter's Church, Buckie

377 PLUSCARDEN ABBEY, ELGIN NJ145576

Benedictine abbey founded 1230, refounded 1948. Famous for its stained glass. Gregorian Chant all services. Benedictine Monks Retreat Houses for men and women. Ecumenical – all welcome. Abbey honey and apiary products on sale in Abbey Gift Shop. Also guidebooks and 'Pluscarden Story', and CDs and tapes of Abbey Chant. Off A96 Forres–Elgin (signed). Sunday Services Mass 8am (English), 10am (Latin). Other Sunday Services 4.45am, 7.30am, 9.05am, 12.35pm, 3.05pm, 4.00pm, 8.00pm

OPEN ALL YEAR 4.45AM–8.45PM

50th anniversary of re-opening, September. Pluscarden Pentecost lectures 'The Holy Spirit' 2–4 June

Roman Catholic WC A

378 GORDON CHAPEL, FOCHABERS NJ3458
Castle Street, Fochabers
Built in 1835 to a design by Archibald Simpson, restored in 1874. Stained glass, Sir Edward Burne-Jones. Joint charge with St Margaret's, Aberlour. North of main square (A96) by Duke Street. Sunday Service 1st Sunday of month 8.30am (9am winter), other Sundays 11.15am
OPEN DAILY DURING DAYLIGHT HOURS
Church is upstairs and not easy of access for the disabled
Scottish Episcopal **A**

379 ST NINIAN'S, TYNET NJ378614
Mill of Tynet, Fochabers
The oldest post-Reformation Catholic church still in use in Scotland. At the request of the Duke of Gordon, 1755, built to resemble a sheepcot in days when it was still an offence to celebrate Mass. Renovated 1957, the long low whitewashed building is still 'a church in disguise'. Saturday Vigil Mass 5.30pm
OPEN BY ARRANGEMENT
Contact Mrs D. Turner, Newlands of Tynet
Roman Catholic **A**

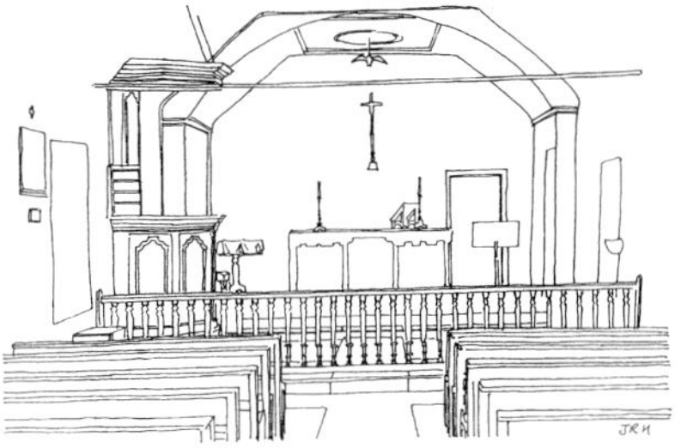

St Ninian's, Tynet by Fochabers

380 ST LAURENCE PARISH CHURCH, FORRES NJ0358
High Street, Forres
Built on a site of Christian worship dating from mid 13th century, today's neo-Gothic building – designed by John Robertson and dedicated in 1906 – is a fine example of the stonemason's craft. The pitch pine ceiling and the stained glass windows by Douglas Strachan and Percy Bacon help to create the special atmosphere of peace and beauty. Font replica of one in Dryburgh Abbey. Sunday Services 10am also 1st Sunday February–November 6.30pm
OPEN MAY–SEPTEMBER MONDAY TO FRIDAY 10AM–12 NOON 2–4PM
Other times by arrangement tel 01309 672260
Church of Scotland WC **B**

381 KNOCKANDO PARISH CHURCH
Award winning design for new church by the Law & Dunbar-Nasmith Partnership, 1993, on the site of an earlier building destroyed by fire in 1990. Sympathetic with the building which it has replaced. The Creation is symbolised in a new stained glass window by Andrew Lawson-Johnson. From A95 Aviemore-Elgin or A941 Dufftown–Elgin, take B9102 Archiestown Knockando. At Cardhu turn right. Church is signposted. Linked with Rothes. Sunday Service 10.30am
OPEN JULY–AUGUST TUESDAY–THURSDAY 2–4.30PM
Church of Scotland

382 ST GREGORY'S CHURCH, PRESHOLME NJ409615

Presholme, Clochan

Built in 1790. A wide rectangular church with harled walls and freestone dressing. The church is adorned with urn finials; its west end is a charming product of 18th-century taste, in which Italian Baroque has been skilfully naturalised to a Banffshire setting. Copy of a painting of St Gregory the Great by Annibale Caracci. Two holy water stoups of Portsoy marble. Sunday Mass occasionally at 6pm

OPEN BY ARRANGEMENT

Contact Mrs D. Slater, 25 Raffan Road, Buckie

Roman Catholic **A**

383 ROTHES PARISH CHURCH

High Street x Seafield Square, Rothes

Built in 1781 with a steeple added in 1870. A traditional Scottish design of the Reformed tradition with the pulpit on the long wall, a three-sided gallery and apse. Pipe organ, 1901, has recently been restored. Linked with Knockando. Sunday Service 12 noon

OPEN JULY–AUGUST MONDAY–FRIDAY 2–4.30PM

Church of Scotland

· Orkney ·

384 ST MAGNUS CHURCH, BIRSAY

The original church was built by Earl Thorfinn *c* 1060 and has been altered and restored several times, most recently in 1985. Stained glass window by Alexander Strachan showing scenes from the life of St Magnus. Inside the church are two 16th & 17th-century tombstones. 17th-century belfry. The Mons Bellus stone is probably from the nearby Bishop's Palace. The church is now maintained by the St Magnus Church Birsay Trust. 20 miles from Kirkwall, across the road from the Earl's Palace. Sunday Service 12 noon on alternate Sundays

OPEN DAILY APRIL–SEPTEMBER

Non-denominational **B**

385 ST MAGNUS CATHEDRAL, KIRKWALL HY449108

Broad Street, Kirkwall

The Cathedral Church of St Magnus the Martyr was founded in 1137 by Earl Rognval Kolson and dedicated to his uncle, Earl Magnus Erlendson. Completed *c* 1500. It contains many items of interest and ranks as one of the finest cathedrals in Scotland. Although it is owned and maintained by Orkney Islands Council, the Society of Friends of St Magnus was formed in 1958 to help raise funds for its preservation. Caretaker on duty. Sunday Service 11.15am

OPEN APRIL–SEPTEMBER MONDAY TO SATURDAY 9AM–6PM SUNDAY 2–6PM, OCTOBER–MARCH MONDAY TO SATURDAY 9AM–1PM & 2–5PM

Closed public holidays and Christmas festive season except for church services

Church of Scotland (side entrance) WC (public nearby) **A**

· Perth & Kinross ·

Local Representative: Col. David Arbuthnott
Trochry Old Manse, Dunkeld, Perthshire PH8 0DY

386 ABERDALGIE AND DUPPLIN PARISH CHURCH
Aberdalgie

Nestling in the Earn Valley on a site of enduring worship for centuries, the present church was built by the Earl of Kinnoull in 1773. A T-plan church of local sandstone features a fine laird's loft and Georgian retiring room. 14th-century Tournai marble Oliphant monument. Sir Robert Lorimer remodelled the interior in 1929. Extensive use of Austrian oak gives the church a sense of peace and simple dignity. Renovations 1994. Signed off B9112, south of Aberdalgie village. Linked with Forteviot. Sunday Service 11.15am

OPEN BY ARRANGEMENT

Contact Revd Colin Williamson tel 01738 625854

Church of Scotland **B**

387 ABERNYTE PARISH CHURCH
Abernyte, by Inchture

The present church was built in 1736 to replace a building of pre-1400, although there may have been a Celtic church here much earlier. Major renovations in 1837 when the present cruciform shape was established. Intricate beams, stained glass and a modern wall hanging of 1992. Signposted from village. Linked with Longforgan and Inchture with Kinnaird. Sunday Sevice 11am

OPEN DURING DAYLIGHT

Church of Scotland **B**

388 ARDOCH PARISH CHURCH NN8309
Feddal Road, Braco

Opened for worship in 1780 as a chapel of ease. The church was originally a rectangular building, the bellcote being added in 1836 and a chancel built on the east end by William Simpson of Stirling in 1890. The most recent addition is the church hall, built 1985. A9 north of Dunblane, take A822 to Braco, turn onto B8033 to Kinbuck and church is on right. Sunday Service 11.30am (1999: Sunday Service 10am)

OPEN BY ARRANGEMENT

Tel 01786 880589

Roman camp nearby

Church of Scotland ♿ 👂 WC **C**

St Magnus Cathedral, Kirkwall

389 ST MARY'S CHURCH, BIRNAM NO0341

Perth Road, Birnam

The main church and clock tower to a design by William Slater, 1858, with north aisle by Norman & Beddoe, 1883. Slater font and cover, Kempe east window, William Morris windows to Burne-Jones designs, 3–bell chime, clock by James Ramsay of Dundee, 1882. Beautifully kept churchyard. On old A9 in centre of village. Sunday Service 9.45am Wednesday 9.30am

OPEN EASTER–MICHAELMAS 9.30AM–6.30PM

Dunkeld & Birnam Arts Festival exhibition, summer concert and choral evensong last week in June

Scottish Episcopal ♿ (via Rectory) 📖 WC **B**

390 DUMBARNEY PARISH CHURCH, BRIDGE OF EARN

Manse Road, Bridge of Earn

Built 1787. Pedimented bellcote added, interior recast and other alterations 1880. Rectangular plan with bow-ended west porch. Off the main street of Bridge of Earn. Sunday Service 9.30am

OPEN 1ST SATURDAYS OF JUNE, JULY & AUGUST & 26, 27, 28 SEPTEMBER 10AM–4PM

Annual Flower Festival 26, 27, 28 September

Church of Scotland WC **C**

391 BRAES OF RANNOCH PARISH CHURCH, BRIDGE OF GAUR NN5056

South Loch Road, Bridge of Gaur

Built in 1907, Peter MacGregor Chalmers. The bellcote is from an earlier building of 1776 and also borne by a church built in 1855 on this site. Rothwell pipe organ, from Urquhart Church, Elgin, rebuilt 1991, David Loosley. B846 Aberfeldy to Bridge of Gaur, and south Loch Rannoch road to Finnart. Sunday Service 10am

OPEN DAILY

Church of Scotland 📖 **B**

392 CLEISH CHURCH NT0998

Cleish

Built on 13th-century site in 1832, with additions 1897. Organ and lights from St Giles, Edinburgh. The hymn 'Jesus, tender Shepherd, hear me' written by former Minister's wife in the Manse. Interesting wall chart and graveyard. Exit 5 M90, Cleish 2 miles. Sunday Service 11.15am

OPEN DAILY 10AM–5PM

Church of Scotland 🦻 **B**

393 COMRIE AND STROWAN PARISH CHURCH NN7722

Burrell Street, Comrie

Built in 1881, George T. Ewing, on a site surrounded by attractive grounds overlooking the River Earn. 16th-century Flemish bell. Organ built 1910 for the London Exhibition. A85. Regular bus service from Perth. Linked with Dundurn. Sunday Service 10am June–September, 10.30am October–May

OPEN DAILY

Church of Scotland ♿ 🦻 📖 WC **C**

394 ST NINIAN'S, CRIEFF NN8621
Comrie Road, Crieff
Placed on the Burrell Street axis, the rectangular church has a broad gabled facade with a
centre tower with a gabled and pinnacled parapet. The old West Church has been refur-
bished to become a modern conference centre. Alterations carried out in 1970. Sunday
Service 9.30am
OPEN ALL YEAR DURING DAYLIGHT HOURS (EXCEPT CHRISTMAS DAY)
Church of Scotland ⑨ ☐ ☕ wc **B**

395 DUNKELD CATHEDRAL NOO242
Cathedral Street, Dunkeld
The Cathedral lies in a superb setting on the banks of the Tay. The restored choir, now used
as the parish church, was completed in 1350. Chapter house (1469) adjacent to choir,
contains a small museum. The tower, ruined nave and south porch are in the care of Historic
Scotland. Just off A9, at west end of Dunkeld. Sunday Service Easter – Remembrance Sunday
11am
OPEN DAILY SUMMER 9.30AM–7PM, WINTER 9.30AM–4PM
Church of Scotland ♿ ⑨ ☐ wc **A**

396 FORTEVIOT PARISH CHURCH (ST ANDREW'S), FORTEVIOT
In an area of historical importance – in the 9th century Kenneth MacAlpin had his palace
here, and a basilica existed from the first half of the 8th century – this church, the third, was
erected in 1778. It was remodelled in the mid 19th century. Celtic bell dated 900AD, one of
five Scottish bronze bells. Medieval carved stones. The font is from the pre-Reformation
church of Muckersie united with Forteviot in 1618. Organ by Hamilton of Edinburgh.
Extensively renovated 1994. Linked with Aberdalgie & Dupplin. Sunday Service 10am
OPEN BY ARRANGEMENT
Contact Revd C. Williamson tel 01738 625854
Church of Scotland **C**

397 FOWLIS WESTER PARISH CHURCH NN9224
The church is a 13th-century building which, and although renovated in 1927 by Jeffrey
Waddell of Glasgow with much Celtic ornament, retains many of the original features
including a "lepers' squint". The Pictish cross under the north wall is evidence of over 1,000
years of Christian worship in the area. Turn off A85 5 miles from Crieff to Fowlis Wester
(signed). Sunday Service 10am
OPEN BY ARRANGEMENT
Contact Mrs McColl tel 01764 683205
Church of Scotland **B**

Fowlis Wester Parish Church

398 ALL SOULS' CHURCH, INVERGOWRIE NO3430

59 Main Street, Invergowrie

Red sandstone church with 140-ft spire, designed by Hippolyte Blanc, 1890. High altar has beautiful Italian marble reredos and crucifix. Lady Chapel contains altar from Rossie Priory Chapel. Sculptured Stations of the Cross. Embroidered wallhanging to celebrate centenary of consecration, 1996. Church hall used for community activities. Services Sunday 10am Sung Eucharist, Wednesday Said Eucharist 10.15am and 6.30pm

OPEN WEEKDAYS DURING SCHOOL TERMS 9AM–4PM

Scottish Episcopal A

399 KILMAVEONAIG CHURCH NN8665

Kilmaveonaig, Blair Atholl

An Episcopal Chapel rebuilt in 1794 by John Stewart on the site of the old parish church of Kilmaveonaig, 1591, and having belonged to the Episcopal Communion without a break since the Revolution. Enlarged 1899. Lorimer reredos added 1912. Old bell, 1629, from Little Dunkeld church. Off A9 to Blair Atholl, opposite Tilt Hotel. Sunday Service 10am

OPEN BY ARRANGEMENT

Key available from Tilt Hotel

Scottish Episcopal B

Kilmaveonaig Church

400 KINCLAVEN PARISH CHURCH NO1538

By Stanley, near Perth

Built 1848 on site of previous church. Mixed Romanesque and Tudor with a narthex at the west end and bellcote at the east end. Churchyard contains the War Memorial lychgate, 1919, by Reginald Fairlie and some table tombs of the 17th century and later. Built into the churchyard wall is the monument to Alexander Cabel (Campbell), Bishop of Brechin, 1608. Sunday Service 9.45am

OPEN BY ARRANGEMENT

Contact Mr Gordon tel 01738710548 or Mr Fraser tel 01250 883264

Church of Scotland WC B

401 THE OLD CHURCH OF RANNOCH, KINLOCH RANNOCH NN6658

South Loch Road, Kinloch Rannoch

A Thomas Telford church of 1829, extensively altered and enlarged 1893. Wooden beamed roof, stained glass window, hour-glass by pulpit. B846 from Aberfeldy, B8019 from Pitlochry. Sunday Service 11.45am

OPEN 3RD SATURDAY IN AUGUST FOR RANNOCH HIGHLAND GATHERING

Other times key from Mrs D. MacDonald, Bridgend Cottage tel 01882 632359

Church of Scotland WC C

402 COLLACE PARISH CHURCH, KINROSSIE NO1832

Kinrossie, by Perth

Early 19th century on site of an earlier church dedicated in 1242. Stained glass window, 1919. Remains of medieval building. Important 17th & 18th-century gravestones. A94 from Perth, signposted from village smithy. Sunday Service 11.15am

OPEN SUNDAYS 21 & 28 JUNE 2–4PM

Church of Scotland B

403 MEIGLE PARISH CHURCH NO2844

The Square, Meigle

Re-built in 1870 by John Carver after fire destroyed the pre-Reformation stone church of 1431. Stands on the ancient site of a turf church, erected by Columban missionaries around 606AD. Fine stone font. Interesting graveyard. Pictish stones in adjacent museum (Historic Scotland). Linked with Kettins. Sunday Service 10am

OPEN 1ST SUNDAY JUNE–AUGUST 2–4PM

Church of Scotland B

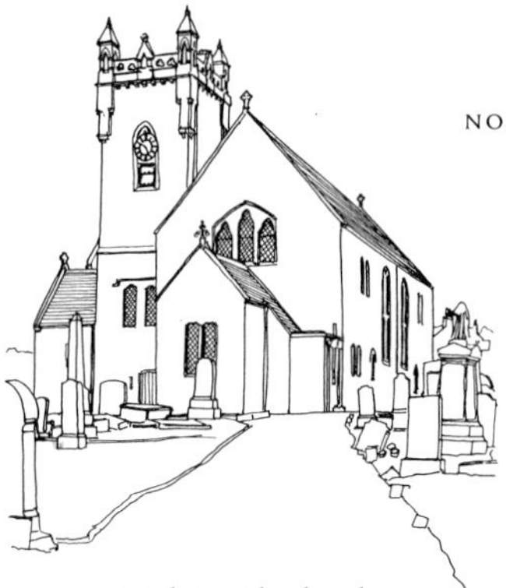

Meigle Parish Church

404 MORENISH CHAPEL

By Killin

Built in 1902 by Aline White Todd in memory of her daughter Elvira who died in childbirth. The central piece of the chapel is the magnificent east window by Tiffany in heavily leaded tracery and sumptuous stained glass showing Moses receiving the ten commandments on Mount Sinai. On A827 Killin–Kenmore. Served by Killin and Ardeonaig. Sunday Service 3pm 1st Sunday of month

Church of Scotland

405 MUTHILL PARISH CHURCH NN8717

Station Road, Muthill, by Crieff

Replacing the 12th-century church (still existing). Built in 1826 in Gothic style to a design by Gillespie Graham, nicknamed 'Pinnacle' Graham by those less enthusiastic for the sprockets of 19th century Gothic. Pulpit canopy similarly sprocketed. A822, 3 miles south of Crieff. Buses from Stirling to Crieff. Sunday Service 11.30am, coffee 11am

OPEN SUNDAY IN AUGUST

Coincides with opening of nearby Drummond Castle Gardens (Scotland's Gardens Scheme)

Church of Scotland B

406 NORTH CHURCH, PERTH

Mill Street, Perth

A pleasant city centre church, built in 1880 by T.L. Watson of Glasgow in Italian Romanesque style. Sunday Service 9.30am 12 noon & 6.30pm, Thursday lunchtime

OPEN BY ARRANGEMENT

Contact Mr G. Weeks tel 01738 635307

Church of Scotland B

407 PITLOCHRY CHURCH NN9458

Church Road, Pitlochry

Built in 1884, C.L. Ower, Dundee. The porch was added in 1995, built of stone from Pitlochry East Church, the East and West congregations having united in 1992. Seating arranged in a part circle around the communion table. Monument to Alexander Duff, 19th-century missionary. Identifiable as 'the church with the clock', 100yds from main street. Sunday Services 9.30am parents and children & 11am

OPEN JUNE–SEPTEMBER MONDAY TO FRIDAY 10AM–12 NOON & 2–4PM

Church of Scotland B

408 DUNDURN PARISH CHURCH, ST FILLANS NN6924

St Fillans

Built 1879. Of particular interest is the medieval stone font. Oak panelling, pulpit and communion table with Celtic knotwork. Set in grounds with striking view across Loch Earn. Linked with Comrie and Strowan. Sunday Service 11.30am June–September, 12 noon October–May

OPEN DAILY FROM EASTER TO OCTOBER

Church of Scotland

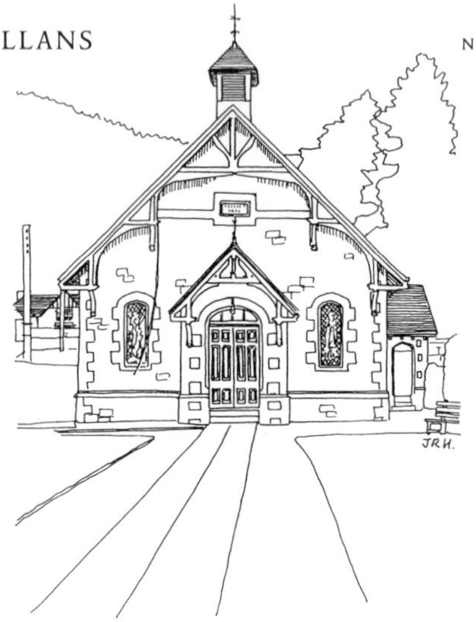

Dundurn Parish Church, St Fillans

409 ST MADOES AND KINFAUNS CHURCH NO1921

Glencarse, near Perth

Built 1799 on the site of earlier churches and refurbished in 1923. T-plan church with laird's gallery. New vestry and entrance hall by David Murdoch of Methven, 1996. Interesting historic graveyard with 18th-century gravestones of sculptural merit. Pictish St Madoes Stone now on display in Perth Museum and Art Gallery. Contemporary embroidered pulpit falls. Sunday Service September–May 11am, June–August 10am

OPEN FIRST SUNDAY OF MONTH JUNE–SEPTEMBER 1–4PM

Church of Scotland B

410 SCONE OLD PARISH CHURCH

Burnside, Scone

Church built in 1286 near to Scone Palace. Moved to present site in 1806, using stone from original building. Mansfield pew presented by Queen Anne of Denmark, 1615. Memorial to David Douglas, botanist, in graveyard. A94 from Perth. 7 bus from Perth. Sunday Service 11am

OPEN SATURDAYS 8 MARCH, 17 MAY, 16 AUGUST & 18 OCTOBER 10AM–12 NOON

Church of Scotland B

411 ST ANDREW'S CHURCH, STRATHTAY NN9153

Strathtay

The chancel was built in 1888 and the nave added in 1919. A vestibule and hall were added in 1982. Heavily carved woodwork on pulpit, lectern and Priest's prayer desk. Lovely stained glass. A free-standing belfry was provided in 1995. In village, over River Tay from Grandtully on A827 between Ballinluig and Aberfeldy. Linked with St Mary's, Birnam. Sunday Service 11.30am

OPEN BY ARRANGEMENT

Key from village shop, Mr J. Taylor

Scottish Episcopal WC **A**

412 TENANDRY CHURCH

Tenandry, Pitlochry

Small country church built in 1836 of stone and slate, and of traditional design. Fine view of the Pass of Killiecrankie from the road above the church. Turn north from B8019 at Garry Bridge, 2 miles north of Pitlochry – signed. Sunday Service 11am

OPEN DAILY

Church of Scotland WC **B**

413 FOSS KIRK, TUMMEL BRIDGE NN7858

South Loch Tummel Road, Tummel Bridge

Founded 625AD by St Chad and used until the Reformation. Fell into disrepair 1580, restored 1821. 1824 Perth bell. Ancient graveyard behind the church with view of Loch Tummel. Linked with Braes of Rannoch and Rannoch. B8019 from Pitlochry to Tummel Bridge, then B846 to Foss. Sunday Services May–September 1st & 3rd Sundays 7pm, October–April 1st Sunday 2.30pm

OPEN DAILY

Church of Scotland **C**

· Renfrewshire ·

Local Representative: Mr Norman MacGilvray
15 Carriagehill Drive, Paisley PA2 6JG

414 HOUSTON & KILLELLAN PARISH CHURCH NS4066

Kirk Road, Houston

Gothic, 1874 by David Thomson, this building is the third on this ancient site. Very good stained glass. Interesting organ. Between Bridge of Weir and Inchinnan. Sunday Service 11am

OPEN SUNDAYS 11AM–1PM

Church of Scotland **B**

415 INCHINNAN PARISH CHURCH (ST CONVAL'S) NS4769

Old Greenock Road, Inchinnan

Sir R. Rowand Anderson's St Conval's Kirk of 1903 was razed to make way for Glasgow Airport, and the present building by Miller and Black, consecrated in 1968, incorporates much of interest and beauty from the earlier church. Celtic and medieval stones, some of which are believed to relate to the Knights of St John. 2 miles west of Renfrew on A8. Sunday Service 10.45am

OPEN THURSDAY DURING TERM TIME NOON–1.30PM

Light lunches available

Church of Scotland ♿ ② ⛪ 📖 ☕ wc

416 JOHNSTONE HIGH PARISH CHURCH NS4263

Quarry Street, Johnstone

An octagonal building of grey sandstone, built in 1792. Clock tower with spire. Stained glass. Historic graveyard. Town centre. Trains from Glasgow every 20 mins. Sunday Service 11am. Songs of Praise 1st Sunday 6.30pm

OPEN THURSDAY TO SATURDAY 10AM–12NOON ALL YEAR

Tours by arrangement at church hall coffee shop

Church of Scotland ♿ ② 📖 ☕ wc **B**

417 KILBARCHAN WEST CHURCH NS4063

Church Street, Kilbarchan

Hall built as the church in 1724 on the site of an earlier church. Present church completed 1901, architect W.H. Howie. Some fine stained glass resited from old church and glass from early 20th century. 3-manual organ built 1904 by William Hill & Sons. On A737 next to Weaver's Cottage. Sunday Services 11am, Wednesdays 10.30 October–May

OPEN EASTER–END SEPTEMBER TUESDAY & THURSDAY 2–4PM

Church of Scotland ♿ ② ⛪ ☐ wc **B**

Johnstone High Parish Church

418 LINWOOD PARISH CHURCH

Blackwood Avenue, Linwood

A spacious red brick building dating from 1965. An earlier church of 1860 existed on another site, demolished in 1976. The furniture and communion silver are from the earlier church. Comtemporary art work includes a large aluminium cross presented by the former Rootes Vehicle Plant. Fine pipe organ, 1957. Sunday Service 9.30am & 11am. Friday 11.30–1.30 during school term

OPEN BY ARRANGEMENT

Contact Mrs F. Dooley tel 01505 331 065

Church of Scotland

419 PAISLEY ABBEY NS4864

Founded in 1163. Early 20th-century restoration of the choir by P. MacGregor Chalmers and Lorimer. Medieval architecture, royal tombs of Marjory Bruce and Robert III, the 10th-century Barochan Cross. Exceptionally fine woodwork by Lorimer, stained glass by Burne-Jones and others. M8, Junction 27, follow signs to Paisley town centre. By train to Paisley, Gilmour Street. Sunday Services 11am, 12.15pm (Holy Communion), 6.30pm

OPEN DAILY MONDAY TO SATURDAY 10AM–3.30PM

Special open days with tower open & guided tours 2 May, 6 June, 4 July, 15 August, 12 September, 17 October. Other details from Abbey office tel 0141 889 7654

Church of Scotland (limited) WC A

420 CASTLEHEAD PARISH CHURCH, PAISLEY

Main Road, Castlehead, Paisley

Built 1781 as the first Relief church in Paisley. Interior renovated 1881. Bishop organ, 1898. Graveyard has graves of Robert Tannahill (local poet), past ministers, merchants and the mass graves of the cholera epidemic. At west end of town, at junction of Castlehead Main Road and Canal Street. Sunday Service 11am

OPEN MAY–SEPTEMBER MONDAY WEDNESDAY FRIDAY 2–4PM

Church of Scotland WC B

421 MARTYRS' CHURCH, PAISLEY

Broomlands Street, Paisley

The church is named after the Paisley martyrs who were executed in 1685. Built 1847 with additions and alterations, including tower and south front in neo-Norman style, 1905, T.G. Abercrombie, architect. Inside are galleries on three sides on cast-iron colonnettes. The pulpit, 18-ft long, has been likened to the bridge of a ship. On A737 west of Paisley centre. Sunday Service 11am

OPEN FRIDAY 10AM–1PM

Church of Scotland WC B

422 NEW JERUSALEM CHURCH, PAISLEY

17 George Street, Paisley

Built for Wesleyan Methodists in 1810, and in use by Swedenborgians since 1860, this is an unusual building with halls on the ground floor and the church upstairs. Three striking stained glass windows by W. & J.J. Kerr, including one designed by Sir Noel Paton. Fine pulpit and communion table. Nearest railway stations Paisley Canal and Paisley Gilmour Street. Sunday Service 11am

OPEN BY ARRANGEMENT

Contact Revd Robert Gill tel 0141 887 4119

Swedenborgian

423 ST JAMES'S CHURCH, PAISLEY

Underwood Road, Paisley

Early French Gothic style to a design by Hippolyte Blanc, largely gifted by Sir Peter Coats, 1884. 200-ft spire. Full peal of bells, rung every Sunday. Father Willis pipe organ, rebuilt J. Walker 1967. Stained glass windows 1904. Landscaped grounds. M8, junction 29, St James interchange. Sunday Service 11am

OPEN MONDAY WEDNESDAY & FRIDAY 10AM–4PM

Also Doors Open Day September 10am–4pm

Contact day centre at rear of church for access

Church of Scotland WC **B**

424 THOMAS COATS MEMORIAL BAPTIST CHURCH, PAISLEY

High Street, Paisley

Built by the Coats Family as a memorial to Thomas Coats. Hippolyte Blanc Gothic, opened May 1894. Beautiful interior, 'by far the grandest of the Paisley churches' (*Groome's Gazetteer*) with carved marble and alabaster. Famous Hill 4-manual pipe organ. On main street going west from Paisley Cross. Sunday Service 11am

OPEN MAY–SEPTEMBER MONDAY WEDNESDAY FRIDAY 2–4PM

Or by arrangement contact Church Secretary tel 0141 889 6690

Baptist WC **A**

425 WALLNEUK NORTH CHURCH, PAISLEY

Abercorn Street, Paisley

Built 1915. Pipe organ by Abbott & Smith, 1931, dedicated to Peter Coats, donor of this church. Its fine oak case was designed by Abercrombie & Maitland, Glasgow and carved and built by Wylie & Lochead, Glasgow. Near town centre. Sunday Service 11am also 1st Sunday in Mossvale Hall 6.30pm. Wednesday 12.30pm

OPEN DOORS OPEN DAY SEPTEMBER

Church of Scotland **A**

426 ST MACHAR'S, RANFURLY NS3865

Kilbarchan Road, Ranfurly, Bridge of Weir

Early Gothic, 1878 by Lewis Shanks, brother of one of the local millowners. The chancel was added, 1910 by Alexander Hislop. Stained glass by J.S. Melville & J. Stewart, 1900, Herbert Hendrie, 1931, William Wilson, 1946, Gordon Webster, 1956. Descriptive booklet by Maurice L. Gaine, 1996. A761 at east end of village. Sunday Service 11am (10.30am July & August)

OPEN FRIDAYS 10AM–12NOON

Bridge of Weir Gala Week in June

Church of Scotland WC

427 RENFREW OLD PARISH CHURCH NS5067

26 High Street, Renfrew

The Church of Renfrew was bestowed by King David on the Cathedral Church of Glasgow in 1136. Within the present lancet Gothic 1862 sanctuary are two late medieval monuments, a hooded vault with recumbent effigies and an altar tomb. In Renfrew town centre. Regular bus services from Glasgow and Paisley. Sunday Services 11.15am & 6.30pm

OPEN DOORS OPEN DAY SEPTEMBER

Church of Scotland WC B

· East Renfrewshire ·

428 WILLIAMWOOD PARISH CHURCH, CLARKSTON NS5757

Seres Road, Clarkston

Built in 1937 as a church extension charge, the church is a fine example of mid-thirties church architecture. Original and somewhat austere interior upgraded and enriched. Historical and other information available. By rail from Glasgow Central to Williamwood or Clarkston, 10 minutes walk from both stations. Bus services from Glasgow to Eaglesham, alight at Clarkston. Sunday Service 11am

OPEN FEBRUARY–JUNE AND SEPTEMBER–DECEMBER WEEKDAYS 9.45AM–12 NOON

Other information tel 0141 638 2091

Church of Scotland

Williamwood Parish Church, Clarkston

429 ORCHARDHILL PARISH CHURCH, GIFFNOCK

Church Road, Giffnock

Church and hall built in Gothic Revival style, H.E. Clifford, 1900. Of local stone with a red tiled roof, squat tower with spiral wooden stair and roof turret. Extensions carried out in 1910 and 1935. Stained glass (1936–86) and wood panelling (1900–35). 2-manual pipe organ, Hill, Norman & Beard. Embroidered pulpit falls 1993. On east side of Fenwick Road, north of Eastwood Toll. Buses from Glasgow Buchanan and trains from Glasgow Central. Sunday Service Winter 11am & 6.30pm, Summer 9.30am & 11am

OPEN BY ARRANGEMENT

Contact Church Officer tel 0141 620 3346 or 638 3604

Church of Scotland B

430 NETHERLEE PARISH CHURCH

Ormonde Avenue, Netherlee, Glasgow

Built in neo-Gothic style of red Dumfriesshire sandstone, Stewart & Paterson 1934. Oak panelling and furnishings beautifully carved. Lovely stained glass. City buses via Clarkston Road. Sunday Services September–May 11am & 6.30pm, June–August 9.30am & 11am

OPEN BY ARRANGEMENT

Contact Mr McVey tel 0141 637 6853

Church of Scotland WC B

431 CALDWELL PARISH CHURCH, UPLAWMOOR NS4355

Neilston Road, Uplawmoor

Simple country church built 1889, William Ingram. Memorial glass sculpture depicting the Trinity, Ralph Cowan 1989. Garden of Remembrance dedicated 1997. Off B736 Barrhead–Irvine. On main street opposite village shop. Sunday Service 11am, Wednesday brief act of worship 12 noon

OPEN DAILY 11AM–3PM

Soup lunch in hall adjacent October to March Friday 12 noon–1.30pm

Church of Scotland WC

Netherlee Parish Church

· Stirling ·

Local Representative: Mr Louis Stott
Browsers' Bookshop, 25 High Street, Dunblane FK15 OEE

432 ABERFOYLE PARISH CHURCH

Loch Ard Road, Aberfoyle

John Honeyman designed this church which sits at the foot of Craigmore and on the banks of the River Forth. 1870, in early-Gothic style, it replaced the old kirk of Aberfoil on the south bank of the river reached by crossing the hump-backed bridge. The new church was enlarged in 1884 to include transepts. The interior is elegant with the minimum of ornamentation. Magnificent roof timbers. Stained glass, including a window by Gordon Webster 1974. 2-manual pipe organ, 1887 by Bryceson Brothers, London. On the B829. Linked with Port of Menteith. Sunday Service 11.15am

OPEN SATURDAY AFTERNOON IN AUGUST FOR CHURCH SALE

Other times contact Mr I. Nicholson tel 01877 382337

Church of Scotland B

433 BALQUHIDDER PARISH CHURCH

Handsome parish church in dressed stone built in 1853, by David Bryce. Inside both a 'Bedell' Bible and a 'Kirk' Bible on display, and an exhibition of the history of the church. Bell donated by Revd Robert Kirk (1644–92), a notable boulder font and the supposed gravestone of St Angus, possibly 9th-century. The ruins of the old parish church are in the graveyard where there are many intriguing carved stones, including that of Rob Roy MacGregor. A84 at Kinghouse. Linked with Killin. Sunday Service 12 noon

OPEN DAILY

Summer Music Sunday evenings in summer months

Church of Scotland B

434 LOGIE KIRK, BLAIRLOGIE NS8396

The tower, square and pedimented and surmounted by an octagonal belfry, was designed by William Stirling of Dunblane, 1805. The remainder of the church, an elegant whinstone box, by McLuckie and Walter of Stirling, 1901. Stained glass windows include one by C.E. Kempe and two modern windows by John Blyth. Fourteen oak panels depicting scenes from the Bible enclose the chancel and pulpit. The ruined Old Kirk of Logie, with its good selection of 17th and 18th-century gravestones, is nearby. In idyllic rural setting at foot of Dumyat and in the shadow of the Wallace Monument. A91, 4 miles north-east of Stirling. Sunday Service 11.30am

OPEN SUNDAYS IN AUGUST 2–5PM

Church of Scotland B

Logie Kirk, Blairlogie

435 HOLY TRINITY PARISH CHURCH, BRIDGE OF ALLAN NS7997

Keir Street, Bridge of Allan

Built in 1860 and enlarged later, the church contains chancel furnishings designed in 1904 by the eminent Scottish architect, Charles Rennie Mackintosh. The church has an attractive timber roof and excellent stained glass windows. On corner with Fountain Road, opposite Shoprite car park. Bus service from Stirling to Royal Hotel–one block. Rail service to Bridge of Allan Station – 10 mins. walk. Sunday Service 11am

OPEN JUNE–SEPTEMBER SATURDAYS 10AM–4PM

Annual opening special event 1st Saturday in June

Church of Scotland **B**

436 ST SAVIOUR'S CHURCH, BRIDGE OF ALLAN

Keir Street, Bridge of Allan

Built in 1857, and later enlarged, St Saviour's forms part of a group of Gothic revival buildings comprising church, hall and rectory by Alexander Ross. West window, Stephen Adam. Pipe organ Forster & Andrews, 1872. By road, bus and rail services, from Stirling. On corner with Fountain Road. Sunday Services 8am Said Eucharist, 1st Sunday 10am Matins, remaining Sundays 10am Sung Eucharist & Sermon

OPEN DURING DAYLIGHT HOURS

Other times apply to the Rectory

Scottish Episcopal **B**

437 GARGUNNOCK PARISH CHURCH NS7094

Manse Brae, Gargunnock

Situated in very beautiful rural location. Village church 1650 on pre-Reformation foundation, renovated 1774 and 1891. Three individual outside stairs to three separate lairds' lofts. Two good 20th-century stained glass windows. War memorial by Lorimer. Mountain indicator. Graveyard. 5 miles west of Stirling off A811. Sunday Service 11.30am

OPEN BY ARRANGEMENT

Contact Mr Brown tel 01786 860629

Church of Scotland **B**

438 KILLIN AND ARDEONAIG PARISH CHURCH

Main Street, Killin

Distinctive white-harled octagonal classical church built in 1744 by the mason Thomas Clark to a design by John Douglas of Edinburgh. Inside it has been altered from a 'wide' church to a 'long' church. The Fillan Room, a small chapel for prayer in the tower, was created in 1990. In front of the church is a monument to Revd James Stewart (1701–96), minister of Killin who first translated the New Testament into Scots Gaelic (published 1763) At the eastern end of the village. Serves Morenish Chapel (see Perth & Kinross); linked with Balquhidder. (Information about Services in Morenish Chapel from Tourist Information by Falls of Dochart in village). Sunday Service 10am

OPEN MAY–OCTOBER DURING DAYLIGHT HOURS

Church of Scotland **B**

439 PORT OF MENTEITH

On the shore of the Lake of Menteith, a church built in 1878 to designs by John Honeyman, on a site of earlier churches with medieval connections. Simple rectangular plan, Gothic style, with square tower containing carillon of eight bells. Victorian pipe organ, probably by Brook. Surrounded by a graveyard and a few minutes walk from the ferry to Inchmahome where the ruined 13th-century Augustinian Priory may be visited. On B8034 beside the Lake Hotel. Linked with Aberfoyle. Sunday Service 10am

OPEN BY ARRANGEMENT

Contact Mr G. Ellis tel 01877 385201

Church of Scotland WC B

440 THE CHAPEL ROYAL, STIRLING CASTLE

There has been a Chapel in the Castle since at least 1117. It became the Chapel Royal of Scotland in the time of James IV in about 1500. The present building was built in 1594 by James VI for the baptism of Prince Henry. It was redecorated in 1629 in advance of the visit in 1633 of Charles I. After being subdivided to serve military uses there was a first phase of restoration in the 1930s, and the latest phase of work was completed in 1996. A large rectangular building with Renaissance windows and a central entrance framed by a triumphal arch along its south front. Notable features include decorative paintings of 1629 by Valentine Jenkin, a modern wagon ceiling reflecting the profile of the original, and modern furnishings, including a communion table cover designed by Malcolm Lochead. Services by arrangement

OPEN APRIL–OCTOBER 9.30AM–6PM, NOVEMBER–MARCH 9.30AM–5PM

Non-denominational (Castle Restaurant) A

Gargunnock Parish Church

441 CHURCH OF THE HOLY RUDE, STIRLING NS7993

St John Street, Stirling

The original parish kirk of Stirling, used for the coronation in 1567 of James VI, at which John Knox preached. Largely built in 15th & 16th centuries. Medieval open-timbered oak roof in nave. Choir and apse added in 1555, the work of John Coutts, one of the greatest master masons of the later middle ages. Notable stained glass. Fine pipe organ, recently restored. Oak choir stalls and canopies, 1965. Historic graveyard. Near to Stirling Castle. On Historic Stirling (open top) bus route. Sunday Service – time varies, see the church noticeboard

OPEN MAY–SEPTEMBER 10AM–5PM

Venue for many concerts

Church of Scotland A

Church of the Holy Rude, Stirling

442 HOLY TRINITY CHURCH, STIRLING

Albert Place, Dumbarton Road, Stirling

One of Sir R. Rowand Anderson's most distinctive churches, 1878, close to Stirling Castle, Old Town and shops. Very close to town centre, on Historic Stirling (open top) bus route. Sunday Services Eucharists 8.30 & 10.30am, Evening prayer 6.30pm

OPEN MORNINGS DAILY

Scottish Episcopal B

· Cumbria ·

443 THE CHURCH OF SCOTLAND IN CARLISLE NY3956

Chapel Street, Carlisle

Built 1834, altered 1979 and extended 1994. A city centre church, the interior is arranged over two floors with halls and kitchen on the ground floor and sanctuary on the first floor. The extension provides three floors housing ecumenical One World Centre, coffee lounge and Fair Trade shop. 2 minutes from main 'Lanes' shopping area and civic centre, 5 minutes from the cathedral, castle and parks, 10 minutes from Tullie House Museum. 2 minutes from bus station in Lowther Street. Sunday Service 11am, also 6.30pm 1st Sunday (except January, July & August)

OPEN MONDAY–FRIDAY 10AM–2PM

Coffee lounge and Fair Trade shop open Monday to Friday 10am–2pm

Church of Scotland A

SCOTLAND'S CHURCHES SCHEME

ENCOURAGES CHURCHES TO:

Open their doors with a welcoming presence · Tell the story of the building, its purpose and the faith which inspired it · Care for visitors in a sensitive & enriching way · Work together with others to make the Church the focus of its community

SUPPORTS CHURCHES WITH:

The annual publication of its comprehensive guidebook – Churches to Visit in Scotland · Free advice on all aspects of visitor welcome, publicity, interpretation & exhibitions · A network of local representatives in direct contact with headquarters · Effective national publicity

Scotland's Churches Scheme gratefully acknowledges financial support from:

BARCAPEL FOUNDATION LTD · THE CRAY TRUST

THE CRUDEN FOUNDATION · THE ESMÉE FAIRBAIRN TRUST

THE INCHCAPE FOUNDATION · STEWART IVORY & CO

THE LLOYDS TSB FOUNDATION · THE McCORQUODALE TRUST

THE MANIFOLD TRUST · THE SIR JAMES MILLER TRUST · THE OPEN CHURCHES TRUST

THE PILGRIM TRUST · THE RUSSELL TRUST

THE A.E.H.SALVESEN TRUST · THE SCOTTISH EPISCOPAL CHURCH

SCOTTISH & NEWCASTLE PLC · THE SCOTTISH TOURIST BOARD

D.C.THOMSON LTD AND

SEVERAL ANONYMOUS PRIVATE BENEFACTORS

For further information about the Scheme and an application form for entry in the 1999 Yearbook, please write to Scotland's Churches Scheme, Dunedin, Holehouse Rd, Eaglesham, Glasgow G76 0JF, tel 01355 302416, fax 01355 303181.

DONATIONS

Please consider making a donation to Scotland's Churches Scheme, either in an individual or corporate capacity, so that this guide may become an indispensable part of the Scottish calendar, and the permanent financial future of the Scheme is secured.

The options include [1] Donations and [2] Donations which generate additional monies through the reclaim of tax already paid by donors such as:

[a] A Deed of Covenant for a minimum of four years (see form overleaf)
[b] Gift Aid through donations of £250 or more
[c] Gifts through the Charities Aid Foundation
[d] Give As You Earn schemes operated by employers, and
[e] Bequests in a will, which are exempt from Inheritance Tax

Information and forms for [b] and [c] may be obtained from Scotland's Churches Scheme, Dunedin, Holehouse Rd, Eaglesham, Glasgow G76 0JF, tel 01355 302416, fax 01355 303181.

· Donation Form ·

I enclose £ as a donation to Scotland's Churches Scheme

Name

Address

Postcode

· Deed of Covenant Form ·

To: Scotland's Churches Scheme Charity No. SC 022868
I,

of *[Address of Covenanter]*

Postcode

promise to pay you for [1] years, or during my lifetime, if shorter, such a sum as, after deduction of income tax at the basic rate, amounts to

[2] £ each year

[3] from *[the date shown below]*

[4] Signed

Date

Witnessed by

Signature of Witness

Address of Witness

Postcode

NOTES

[1] Enter the period of the covenant which must be longer than three years
[2] Enter the amount you will be paying to the charity
[3] Delete as appropriate. If you chose to enter an actual date it must not be earlier than the date you sign the deed
[4] You should sign the deed and enter the date you actually sign it in the presence of a witness who should see you sign and then immediately sign as witness where shown

After completion, please send this form and remittance to: Scotland's Churches Scheme, Dunedin, Holehouse Rd, Eaglesham, Glasgow G76 0JF Tax reference ED729/94

Scotlands Garden Scheme

Opening gardens is hard work! But it does at least ensure that your garden is tidy for one part of the year! This is not, of course, the only advantage as it also enables you to give an enormous amount of pleasure to a large number of people, and at the same time support a charity of your own choice. This policy is unique to Scotland's Gardens Scheme, as we actively encourage our owners to pick any registered charity of their choice to which up to 40% of their day's opening takings may be donated. In 1996, 142 charities received donations from garden owners in this way, and this included over 20 churches throughout Scotland.

There must be many churches needing funds for repairs, and what better way to obtain this funding than by encouraging a local garden owner to open under the Scheme, and then pick the church as their choice of charity. We welcome gardens of all sizes, and very often the smaller garden is a very popular attraction as the visitor can readily identify it with their own. A number of gardens opening in the village on the same day for us is also becoming more popular, or small groups of gardens joining together. Our local organisers will help to make the opening a success and hopefully provide a lot of fun as well.

Last year we had a most successful art exhibition, and this year we are running a photographic competition which is open to all our visitors. Full details are in the latest edition of *Gardens of Scotland*, which we hope you will buy and visit many of the 300 gardens listed.

the national association of NADFAS decorative & fine arts societies

Church Recorders

Church Recorders, part of the National Association of Decorative and Fine Arts Societies (NADFAS) were formed in England in 1973 to provide written and photographic records of the furnishings and some of the fabric in parish churches. The records are invaluable for conservation work and in cases of theft and vandalism. The records are confidential, and are given to the church and other specific authorities, including the Art Library of the Victoria and Albert Museum and the National Library of Scotland. Church Recorders are volunteers and must be members of NADFAS.

The first completed record in Scotland – Maxton Kirk in the Borders – is now in the possession of the church and the relevant authorities. A second church in the Borders is now being undertaken. Stirling Church Recorders with the much larger Church of the Holy Rude, expect to complete their record within two years.

Many churches of all denominations contain wonderful 19th and 20th-century stained glass, fine interior architectural features, historically interesting memorials and many other important artefacts. Church recorders can ensure that all these items are put on permanent record; the public can be made more aware of much that is of interest, thus encouraging more visitors and a wider appreciation of the importance of preservation and conservation in the Churches of Scotland.

Further information can be obtained from the Chairman of Church Recorders, NADFAS House, 8 Guildford Street, London WCIN IDT.

· Churches to Visit in Scotland 1999 ·

To: The Director, Scotland's Churches Scheme,
Dunedin, Holehouse Road, Eaglesham, Glasgow G76 0JF.
Tel 01355 302416 Fax 01355 303181
Web site: http: //churchnet.ucsm.ac.uk/scotchurch/

Please send me details and an application form for entry in the 1999 Guidebook

Name

Address

Postcode

Name & Address of Church

Postcode

Further copies of the 1998 Guidebook are available from the above at £4.50 including postage.

THE OPEN CHURCHES TRUST

When Andrew Lloyd Webber in July 1994 launched the Open Churches Trust, he knew that the Trust could only hope to be a catalyst for something he felt needed to become a nation-wide crusade to return the best of our places of worship to the people.

The huge number of listed Grade I buildings, which had to be kept locked between services, meant that, initially at least, the Trust could only plant its corn-seed and hope that the culture of having these wonderful buildings open for the public to use and enjoy would spread.

The discovery of Scotland's Churches Scheme as a well-established and rapidly growing institution was like manna from heaven, because this immediately removed the burden of all the wonderful churches in Scotland from the Trust's area of work; it was therefore a great pleasure to form a close link, exchange information and help with funding.

The Trust continues its expansion and in 1997 opened 20 more churches in Wales, Birmingham and Gloucestershire. In 1998 some 22 churches will be opened in Norfolk, Derbyshire and Lincolnshire.

The achievements of Scotland's Churches Scheme and this Trust are now being talked about and our open places are seeing increased numbers of visitors. No person could visit any of the places now open without not only becoming interested in their structure, but also being astounded by the uniqueness of each and its history.

We are blessed in our places of worship which represent the most continuous story of our heritage. We are very privileged to be able to enjoy it.

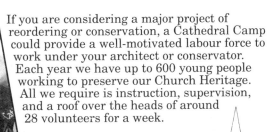

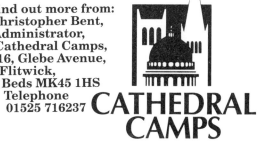

Please note, the references given are to entry numbers **not** pages numbers.

Aberdeen

1 The Cathedral of Our Lady of the Assumption
2 The Chapel of the Convent of St Margaret of Scotland
3 Ferryhill Parish Church
4 Gilcomston South Church
5 Kirk of St Nicholas
6 Newhills Church
7 Rosemount Church
8 St Andrew's Cathedral
9 St Columba's Parish Church
10 St Machar's Cathedral
11 St Margaret of Scotland
12 St Mary's Church

Aberdeenshire

13 St Ternan's Church, Arbuthnott
14 Birse and Feughside Parish Church, Ballogie
15 Banff Parish Church
16 St James's Church, Cruden Bay
17 St Mary on the Rock, Ellon
18 Fintry Parish Church
19 Bervie Parish Church, Inverbervie
20 St Philip's Catterline
21 Finzean Church
22 St Drostan, Insch
23 King David of Scotland Episcopal Church, Inverbervie
24 Macduff Parish Church
25 St Matthew & St George, Oldmeldrum
26 Old Seminary, Scalan
27 St James the Great, Stonehaven
28 Strachan Church
29 All Saints', Whiterashes
30 All Saints', Woodhead of Fetterletter

Angus

31 St Vigean's Church, Arbroath
32 Brechin Cathedral
33 Lowson Memorial Church, Forfar
34 St John the Evangelist, Forfar
35 Glen Prosen Church
36 Kettins Parish Church, by Coupar Angus
37 Kirriemuir Old Parish Church
38 St Mary's Church, Kirriemuir
39 St Margaret's Church, Lunanhead
40 Holy Trinity Church, Monifieth
41 Montrose Old Church

Argyll & Bute

42 St James' Church, Ardbrecknish
43 Church of the Holy Spirit, Ardchattan
44 Kilmeny Parish Church, Ballygrant, Isle of Islay
45 Kilbrandon Kirk, Balvicar, Isle of Seil
46 Kilarrow Parish Church, Bowmore, Isle of Islay
47 Highland Parish Church, Campbeltown
48 Lorne and Lowland Church, Campbeltown
49 Cardross Parish Church
50 Colintraive Church
51 St Oran's Church, Connel
52 Dunoon Baptist Church Centre
53 Dunoon Old and St Cuthbert's Church
54 St John's Church, Dunoon
55 Gigha and Cara Parish Church
56 Glenaray & Inveraray Parish Church
57 Kilmodan Church, Glendaruel
58 St Michael and All Angels, Helensburgh
59 The West Kirk of Helensburgh
60 Iona Abbey
61 Iona Parish Church
62 Kilberry Parish Church
63 Kilfinan Parish Church
64 Kilmartin Parish Church
65 Kilmun Parish Church, St Munn's
66 St Finan's Church, Kinlochmoidart
67 Kiel Church, Lochaline
68 Lochgoilhead & Kilmorich Parish Church
69 Luss Parish Church
70 Cathedral Church of St John the Divine, Oban
71 Tarbert Parish Church
72 Kilchattan Kirk, Toberonochy, Isle of Luing

East Ayrshire

73 Catrine Parish Church
74 Galston Parish Church (St Peter's)
75 Henderson Parish Church, Kilmarnock
76 Holy Trinity Church, Kilmarnock
77 Laigh Kirk, Kilmarnock
78 St Marnock's Parish Church, Kilmarnock
79 St Maur's Glencairn Parish Church, Kilmaurs
80 Mauchline Parish Church
81 Sorn Parish Church
82 St Columba's Parish Church, Stewarton

North Ayrshire

83 Beith High Church
84 The Cathedral of the Isles, Cumbrae
85 St Margaret's Parish Church, Dalry
86 St Andrew's Parish Church (Ferguson Memorial), Irvine
87 The Auld Kirk of Kilbirnie
88 The Abbey Church, Kilwinning
89 Lamlash Parish Church, Isle of Arran
90 Clark Memorial Church, Largs
91 St Columba's Parish Church, Largs
92 St Cuthbert's Parish Church, Saltcoats

South Ayrshire

93 Alloway Parish Church
94 Holy Trinity Church, Ayr
95 Ballantrae Parish Church
96 Barr Parish Church
97 Dundonald Parish Church
98 Sacred Hearts of Jesus and Mary, Girvan
99 Glenapp Church
100 Kirkmichael Parish Church
101 Kirkoswald Parish Church
102 Straiton Parish Church (St Cuthbert's)
103 Our Lady and St Meddan Church, Troon
104 Portland Parish Church, Troon

Borders

105 Bedrule Church
106 Bowden Kirk
107 Broughton, Glenholm & Kilbucho Parish Church
108 Coldstream Parish Church
109 Crailing Kirk
110 Denholm Church
111 Drumelzier Kirk, by Broughton
112 Eckford Kirk, by Kelso
113 Galashiels Old Parish Church & St Paul's
114 St Peter's Church, Galashiels
115 St Cuthbert's Church, Hawick
116 Hobkirk Parish Church, by Bonchester Bridge

117 Hownam Parish Church, by Morebattle
118 Kelso North
119 Kelso Old Parish Church
120 St Andrew's Church, Kelso
121 The Kirk of Yetholm, Kirk Yetholm
122 Legerwood Parish Church
123 Linton Kirk & Hoselaw Chapel, by Morebattle
124 Holy Trinity, Melrose
125 Minto Church
126 Morebattle Parish Church
127 Newtown Church
128 Oxnam Kirk
129 Peebles Old Parish Church
130 Roxburgh Parish Church
131 Southdean Parish Church, by Hawick
132 Stobo Kirk
133 Tweedsmuir Kirk
134 St Mungo's Church, West Linton

Clackmannan

135 Alloa Parish Church (St Mungo's)
136 St John's Church, Alloa
137 Clackmannan Parish Church
138 St James the Great, Dollar

Dumfries & Galloway

139 St Columba's Church, Annan
140 Carsphairn Parish Church
141 Closeburn Parish Church
142 Colvend Parish Church, by Dalbeattie
143 Kirkbean Parish Church
144 Kirkmabreck Parish Church, Creetown
145 St Peter's Church, Dalbeattie
146 Dalton Kirk
147 Greyfriars Church, Dumfries
148 St George's, Dumfries
149 Durisdeer Parish Church
150 Hightae Kirk
151 St Mungo Parish Church, Kettleholm
152 Monigaff Parish Church, Minnigaff
153 Kells Parish Church, New Galloway
154 Penninghame St John's Parish Church, Newton Stewart
155 Dalry Parish Church, St John's Town of Dalry
156 Southwick Parish Church, by Dumfries
157 Kirkcowan Parish Church
158 St Ninian's Priory Church, Whithorn
159 Wigtown Parish Church

East Dunbartonshire

160 Baldernock Parish Church
161 Campsie Parish Church, Lennoxtown
162 St David's Memorial Park Church, Kirkintilloch
163 St Cyprian's Church, Lenzie

West Dunbartonshire

164 St Mungo's Church, Alexandria
165 Alexandria Parish Church, Balloch
166 New Kilpatrick Parish Church, Bearsden
167 Kilbowie St Andrew's Parish Church, Clydebank
168 Riverside Parish Church, Dumbarton
169 The Church of Kilmaronock

Dundee

170 Dundee Parish Church (St Mary's)
171 Meadowside St Paul's Church
172 St Andrew's Cathedral
173 St Andrew's Parish Church
174 St John the Baptist Church
175 St Mary's Church, Broughty Ferry
176 St Paul's Cathedral
177 St Peter's Free Church
178 St Salvador's Church
179 The Steeple Church
180 Stobswell Parish Church

Edinburgh

181 Augustine United Church
182 Barclay Church
183 Blackhall United Free Church
184 Broughton St Mary's Parish Church
185 Canongate Kirk
186 Carrick Knowe Parish Church
187 Colinton Parish Church (St Cuthbert's)
188 Corstorphine Old Parish Church
189 Corstorphine United Free Church
190 Cramond Kirk
191 Dalmeny Parish Church (St Cuthbert's)
192 Davidson's Mains Parish Church
193 Duddingston Kirk
194 Edinburgh Methodist Mission
195 Edinburgh Seventh-day Adventist Church
196 Greenside Parish Church
197 Greyfriars Tolbooth & Highland Kirk
198 St Philip's, Joppa
199 Kirk O'field Parish Church
200 Kirkliston Parish Church
201 Ebenezer United Free Church, Leith
202 Leith Methodist Church
203 North Leith Parish Church
204 South Leith Parish Church
205 Liberton Kirk
206 Liberton Northfield Parish Church
207 Magdalen Chapel
208 Nicolson Square Methodist Church
209 Old St Paul's
210 Priestfield Parish Church
211 Queensferry Parish Church, South Queensferry
212 Priory Church of St Mary of Mt Carmel, South Queensferry
213 Ratho Parish Church
214 Reid Memorial Church
215 Sacred Heart Church
216 St Andrew's and St George's Parish Church
217 St Andrew's Orthodox Chapel
218 St Barnabas Episcopal Church
219 St Bennet's
220 St Columba by the Castle
221 St Cuthbert's Parish Church
222 St George's West Church
223 St John the Evangelist
224 St Margaret's Chapel, Edinburgh Castle
225 St Margaret's Parish Church
226 St Mary's Episcopal Cathedral
227 St Mary, Star of the Sea, Leith
228 St Michael's and All Saints
229 Viewforth St David and St Oswald
230 Wardie Parish Church

Falkirk

231 St Catherine's Church, Bo'ness
232 Carriden Church, Bo'ness
233 Brightons Parish Church
234 Falkirk Old & St Modan's Parish Church
235 St Mary's Church, Grangemouth

Fife

236 St Columba's Church, Aberdour
237 Anstruther Parish Church
238 Burntisland Parish Church
239 St Serf's Church, Burntisland
240 Crail Parish Church
241 Culross Abbey
242 St James the Great Church, Cupar
243 St John's Parish Church, Cupar
244 Dalgety Parish Church, Dalgety Bay
245 Dunfermline Abbey
246 St Margaret's Memorial Church, Dunfermilne
247 Falkland Parish Church
248 St Luke the Evangelist, Glenrothes
249 St Peter's Parish Church, Inverkeithing
250 St Peter's Episcopal Church, Inverkeithing
251 Kirkcaldy Old Parish Church
252 St Brycedale, Kirkcaldy
253 St Mary, Mother of God, Leslie
254 St Athernase Church, Leuchars
255 Church of the Holy Name, Oakley
256 Rosyth Methodist Church
257 All Saints, St Andrews
258 Hope Park Church, St Andrews
259 St Andrew's Church, St Andrews
260 St Monans Parish Church
261 Wemyss Parish Church
262 The Church At West Wemyss

Glasgow

263 Adelaide Place Baptist Church
264 Battlefield East Parish Church
265 Carmunnock Parish Church
266 Cathedral Church of St Luke
267 Cathedral Church of St Mungo
268 Croftfoot Parish Church
269 Garnethill Synagogue
270 Glasgow International Airport Chapel
271 Govan Old Parish Church (St Constantine's)
272 High Carntyne Parish Church
273 Hillhead Baptist Church
274 Hyndland Parish Church
275 Jordanhill Parish Church
276 St John's Renfield, Kelvindale
277 Kelvinside Hillhead Parish Church
278 King's Park Parish Church
279 Lansdowne Parish Church
280 St James's Parish Church, Pollok
281 Queen's Park Baptist Church
282 Renfield St Stephen's Parish Church and Centre
283 St Aloysius Church
284 St Alphonsus Church
285 St Bride's Church
286 St Columba's Church
287 St Mary's Cathedral
288 St Mungo's Church
289 St Ninian's Church, Pollokshields
290 St Vincent Street – Milton Free Church
291 Shawlands United Reformed Church
292 Sherbrooke St Gilbert's Church, Pollokshields
293 Shettleston Methodist Church
294 Shettleston Old Parish Church
295 University Memorial Church
296 Wellington Church
297 Woodlands Methodist Church

Highlands & Islands

298 St Mary's Church, Beauly
299 Croick Church
300 Dornoch Cathedral
301 St Mary's Church, Eskadale
302 Fearn Abbey
303 St Benedict's Abbey Church, Fort Augustus
304 Fort George Chapel
305 Gairloch Free Church
306 St Mary and St Finan, Glenfinnan
307 Old High Church, Inverness
308 St Andrew's Cathedral, Inverness
309 St Mary's Church, Inverness
310 St Stephen's, Inverness
311 Lairg Parish Church
312 Lochcarron Parish Church (West Church)
313 Our Lady & St Bean, Marydale
314 Nairn Old Parish Church
315 St Moluag, Eorropaidh, Ness
316 Pitfure Church
317 St Callan's Church, Rogart
318 St John the Baptist Church, Rothiemurchus
319 St Peter's & St Andrew's Church, Thurso

Inverclyde

320 St Ninian's Church, Gourock
321 Kilmacolm Old Kirk

North Lanarkshire

322 New Monkland Parish Church, Airdrie
323 Overtown Parish Church
324 Stepps Parish Church

South Lanarkshire

325 Biggar Kirk
326 Bothwell Parish Church
327 Cambuslang Old Parish Church
328 Dalserf Parish Church
329 Drumclog Memorial Kirk
330 Glasford Parish Church
331 Hamilton Old Parish Church
332 St Nicholas Parish Church, Lanark
333 Lesmahagow Old Parish Church
334 Rutherglen Old Parish Church
335 St Columbkille's Church, Rutherglen
336 Avendale Old Parish Church, Strathaven
337 Strathaven East Parish Church

East Lothian

338 Aberlady Parish Church
339 Athelstaneford Parish Church
340 Bolton Parish Church
341 Cockenzie Methodist Church
342 Dirleton Kirk
343 Dunbar Methodist Church
344 Dunbar Parish Church
345 St Anne's Church, Dunbar
346 Prestonkirk Parish Church, East Linton
347 Saltoun Parish Church, East Saltoun
348 Yester Parish Church, Gifford
349 Gullane Parish Church (St Andrew's)
350 St Adrian's, Gullane
351 Holy Trinity Church, Haddington
352 St Mary's Collegiate Church, Haddington
353 Humbie Kirk
354 Parish Church of St Michael's, Inveresk
355 Musselburgh Congregational Church
356 Abbey Church, North Berwick
357 St Baldred's Church, North Berwick

358 Pencaitland Parish Church
359 Chalmers Memorial Church, Port Seton
360 Stenton Parish Church
361 Tranent Methodist Church
362 St Mary's Parish Church, Whitekirk
363 Whittingehame Parish Church

Midlothian

364 Crichton Collegiate Church
365 St Mary's Church, Dalkeith
366 St Nicholas Buccleuch Parish Church, Dalkeith
367 Penicuik South Church
368 St James the Less, Penicuik
369 Rosslyn Chapel (St Matthew's), Roslin

West Lothian

370 St Michael's Parish Church, Linlithgow
371 Livingston Village Kirk
372 Kirk of Calder, Mid Calder
373 Polbeth Harwood Parish Church, West Calder
374 Torphichen Kirk

Moray

375 St Margaret of Scotland, Aberlour
376 St Peter's Church, Buckie
377 Pluscarden Abbey, Elgin
378 Gordon Chapel, Fochabers
379 St Ninian's, Tynet, by Fochabers
380 St Laurence Parish Church, Forres
381 Knockando Parish Church
382 St Gregory's Church, Presholme
383 Rothes Parish Church

Orkney

384 St Magnus Church, Birsay
385 St Magnus Cathedral, Kirkwall

Perth & Kinross

386 Aberdalgie & Dupplin Parish Church, Aberdalgie
387 Abernyte Parish Church
388 Ardoch Parish Church, Braco
389 St Mary's Church, Birnam
390 Dumbarney Parish Church, Bridge of Earn
391 Braes of Rannoch Parish Church, Bridge of Gaur
392 Cleish Church
393 Comrie and Strowan Parish Church
394 St Ninian's, Crieff
395 Dunkeld Cathedral
396 Forteviot Parish Church (St Andrew's)
397 Fowlis Wester Parish Church
398 All Souls' Church, Invergowrie
399 Kilmaveonaig Church
400 Kinclaven Parish Church, by Stanley
401 The Old Church of Rannoch, Kinloch Rannoch
402 Collace Parish Church, Kinrossie
403 Meigle Parish Church
404 Morenish Chapel, by Killin
405 Muthill Parish Church
406 North Church, Perth
407 Pitlochry Church
408 Dundurn Parish Church, St Fillans
409 St Madoes and Kinfauns Church
410 Scone Old Parish Church
411 St Andrew's Church, Strathtay
412 Tenandry Church
413 Foss Kirk, Tummel Bridge

Renfrewshire

414 Houston & Killellan Parish Church
415 Inchinnan Parish Church (St Conval's)
416 Johnstone High Parish Church
417 Kilbarchan West Church
418 Linwood Parish Church
419 Paisley Abbey
420 Castlehead Parish Church, Paisley
421 Martyrs' Church, Paisley
422 New Jerusalem Church, Paisley
423 St James's Church, Paisley
424 Thomas Coats Memorial Baptist Church, Paisley
425 Wallneuk North Church, Paisley
426 St Machar's, Ranfurly
427 Renfrew Old Parish Church

East Renfrewshire

428 Williamwood Parish Church, Clarkston
429 Orchardhill Parish Church, Giffnock
430 Netherlee Parish Church
431 Caldwell Parish Church, Uplawmoor

Stirling

432 Aberfoyle Parish Church
433 Balquhidder Parish Chruch
434 Logie Kirk, Blairlogie
435 Holy Trinity Parish Church, Bridge of Allan
436 St Saviour's Church, Bridge of Allan
437 Gargunnock Parish Church
438 Killin & Ardeonaig Parish Church
439 Port of Menteith Parish Church
440 The Chapel Royal, Stirling Castle
441 Church of the Holy Rude, Stirling
442 Holy Trinity Church, Stirling

Cumbria

443 The Church of Scotland In Carlisle